The Referendum Roundabout

Kieron O'Hara

SOCIETAS
essays in political
& cultural criticism

imprint-academic.com

Copyright © Kieron O'Hara, 2006

The moral rights of the author have been asserted.
No part of any contribution may be reproduced in any form
without permission, except for the quotation of brief passages
in criticism and discussion.

Published in the UK by Societas
Imprint Academic, PO Box 200, Exeter EX5 5YX, UK

Published in the USA by Societas
Imprint Academic, Philosophy Documentation Center
PO Box 7147, Charlottesville, VA 22906-7147, USA

ISBN-10   1 84540 040 2
ISBN-13   9781845400408

A CIP catalogue record for this book is available from the
British Library and US Library of Congress

Contents

	Preface	1
1	Non!	4
2	Ted Takes Us In: Will Harold Bring Us Out?	16
3	Referendums, Practice and Theory	26
4	The Rules	37
5	The Yes Camp	48
6	The No Camp	59
7	The Campaign	72
8	The Results	84
9	The Aftermath I: The European Question	92
10	The Aftermath II: Referendums and the Constitution	102
	Further Reading	109
	Index	111

Preface

For over a decade, Britain has lived under the shadow of a referendum. Great issues of state, ranging from the ratification of the Maastricht Treaty, Britain's joining of a single currency and signing up to the proposed EU constitution have been the subject of promises or arguments that they should be decided by a single-issue nationwide plebiscite. At the same time, smaller regions and some cities and towns of the United Kingdom have actually been consulted with respect to alternative systems of government. Decision by referendum, particularly when questions of governance themselves are raised, often seems less controversial and more straightforward than via the standard political process.

But do we really know how controversial referendums work? In science, the abstraction process is conceptually very simple; generate observations and experiments, and assess theories against that background. There is no such simplicity in constitutional politics. There has been, in the United Kingdom, a single national referendum on a non-trivial issue; in 1975, the people were consulted about the continuation of membership of the European Economic Community.

My aim in this essay is to examine the events of 1975 and their historical background to try to generate a few thoughts about the advantages and disadvantages of the use of large-scale referendums in the narrow context of the United Kingdom. Of course, the conclusions I reach will of necessity be hedged with the caveat that the relevant sample size is 1.

Nevertheless, this single case study is surely suggestive of the problems and simplifications implicit in using a plebiscite to make complex and far-reaching decisions. Referendums are regularly called for, have been used fairly frequently in regions of the United Kingdom since 1997, and would certainly have been implemented at the national level in 2006 had the French supported the EU constitution. Whether one supports the use of a referendum to decide whether the UK joins the euro zone, or signs the EU constitution, or continues to ban hunting, the abstract question of the place of referendums in the informal British constitution remains pressing. The process of democratic consultation on a single issue is supposed, by supporters of a referendum, to lend legitimacy to the outcome. There are interesting philosophical arguments both for and against that supposition, but surely more telling is the concrete experience of an actual referendum. Was 1975 a high spot for inclusive, democratic politics? Did the arguments shine through the rough-and-tumble? If not, then surely the proponents of referendums have a lot of explaining to do, however polished their arguments are in the abstract.

The argument of this essay, as it unfolds, will be a combination of historical narrative, and constitutional description and theory. Under the first heading I shall discuss the development of the EEC, and the repeated attempts of Britain to join it, the context that explains so much of the conduct of 1975 (Chapters One and Two), the two coalitions of campaigners which assembled in 1975 (Chapters Five and Six), the conduct of the campaign (Chapter Seven), the results (Chapter Eight), and the post-1975 history of the European question (Chapter Nine). Under the second I shall discuss the use of referendums in Britain and elsewhere prior to 1975, and the theoretical cases for and against (Chapter Three), the rules of 1975, and the process of their creation (Chapter Four), and the use of referendums after the 1975 experience (Chapter Ten).

A few final preliminaries. First of all, let me thank Andrew Denham for comments and discussions of the manuscript and issues raised, and Anthony Freeman and Imprint Academic for all their help. Secondly, let me respond to one of the more frequent remarks that people make to me: I use the plural 'referendums' as opposed to 'referenda', following David Butler, who justifies the choice by advice from the editors of the Oxford English Dictionary. Although my Latin is close enough to zero to prevent me from properly appreciating their reasoning, I can recognise a convincing argument from authority when I see one.

And thirdly, in many places in this book I have a little fun with the bizarre behaviour and strange decisions of the politicians of the day. There is nothing wrong with pointing out the oddness of many of our rulers. But let me affirm my belief that politicians of all parties belong to a much-maligned species, which (at least in Britain) does a creditable job, under conditions of uncertainty and rapid change, with remarkably little corruption, in return for comparatively low recompense and outrageous intrusion into private life. I would not want this book to be seen as part of the general trend towards distrust of and disillusion with politics. Indeed, an important part of my thesis is that politicians should be less wary of taking decisions, at least when bold decision-making is required.

Chapter One
Non!

Euro-Vision, Anglo-Disdain

The positive vision of a united Europe has a long pedigree from the Romans to Charlemagne to Napoleon, thanks to geography (there are relatively few natural frontiers in Europe, and correspondingly few barriers to the expansion of booming nations), ego and logic (why have lots of tiny states with lots of different systems of money, measurement, etc, when you could have one big one run on streamlined administrative lines?). All schemes overreached, and failed.

The united Europe that has grown today was founded on the negative idea of the failure of the nation-state system and the need to prevent war. The 'Great Powers' theory of diplomacy allowed big nations to pursue aggressive policies towards each other, as long as the network of alliances and treaties between them stopped any one of them getting more powerful than the others. This was a truly terrible theory; all that can be said for it is that it kept peace in Europe, except when there were wars.

The worst point of friction was in the West of the continent. Germany, new-minted and efficient, and France, slowly crumbling but acutely conscious of its heritage and the universality of its founding principles, proved to be too big to share the schoolyard. Germany never had much trouble rolling over its arrogant and complacent enemy, but its aggression meant that effective coalitions could be formed against it. The complete lack of wisdom of statesmen didn't help; in 1918, France disastrously insisted on impossible conditions for German surrender. It took Germany a mere couple of decades to engage France again.

1945 saw a little more far-sightedness. It was held, not unreasonably, that the Great Power system had failed and a new order should link European states so inextricably that war would be unthinkable. The main theorist of this view was Jean Monnet, who had indeed suggested the idea as early as 1940, and the cheerleader-in-chief was

Britain's wartime Prime Minister Winston Churchill. Churchill, rejected by the electorate in 1945, spent an amiable six years as leader of the opposition being an international statesman and celebrity, happily upstaging Clement Attlee by coming to a rapid and eloquent understanding of the post war settlement.

But though Britain was sympathetic, it was not involved, and the union that gradually emerged from a decade and more of painstaking negotiation and institution-building was centred around conservative *Mitteleuropa*. With the lack of official British input into the negotiation process, the idea gradually developed of a European Community as a superstate based around the Rhineland that would be a Catholic buffer against the rise of communism.

The European Union as we know it came into being in 1957, with the ratification of the Treaty of Rome. The original proposal from Dutch Foreign Minister Jacques Beyen was for a customs union with full free trade, but no-one thought that France would drop its protectionist instincts, and it didn't. Free trade was only applicable to vulgar industry; and although national barriers for agriculture were dropped, free competition was not implemented. Instead food prices were to be maintained, and farmers kept artificially solvent, by an executive based in Brussels. The European Economic Community was born on 25th March 1957, with France, West Germany, Italy, Belgium, the Netherlands and Luxembourg ('the Six'). The British dubbed it the 'Common Market', the difference in terminology—'community' v 'market'—hinting at a difference in understanding that persists, with malign results, half a century later.

There were immediate arguments about whether other countries should be allowed to join. The German Christian Democrats, for example, were happy having united the Catholic centre of Europe and wanted to go no further. Socialists worried that a right wing majority would try to bring in fascist Spain and Portugal. On the other hand, more idealistic feeling supported the idea of a club open to all. The compromise was a clause in the preamble of the Treaty of Rome that invited other countries to join, tempered by strict procedures for evaluating a bid, including provision of a veto for all the member states.

So was created a *cordon bleu* recipe for trouble.

The British Inferiority Complex

All should have seemed tickety-boo. Europe had implemented an imaginative plan to end war, and as we know with hindsight the

Community succeeded admirably in that fundamental aim. The British, who would have preferred a looser free trade area, still benefited from strong commercial connections with the newly expanded market. Furthermore, Britain had many ties of commerce and emotion with the countries of the Commonwealth and Empire, and joining the EEC (which promoted freer trade within its borders, but erected barriers against the rest of the world) might have disrupted those. So the good result for Europe should have translated into a positive outcome for Britain.

But it didn't. Just as the Europeans were going their own way without the benefits (dubious or otherwise) of British patronage, and devising a regime in their own interests, the British got cold feet. The Empire was collapsing, and British-Commonwealth trading relations were looking decidedly less favourable. A rival European Free Trade Area (EFTA — the British forgot their antipathy to initials in this case), set up by Britain and others looked like a pale imitation of the Common Market. The economic situation was worsening. In the Autumn of 1960, a special budget had to be brought in to stop a run on the pound. In the wider world, too, Britain looked less like one of the WWII victors; the Suez debacle loomed large in British culture and politics, a demonstration of the new impotence.

And while Britain stagnated under Harold Macmillan, Europe boomed. The post-war British inferiority complex began to kick in, and the suspicion started to spread that maybe the foreigners had got it right — or even if not, to be in their club would be better than being out of it.

Macmillan finally announced a formal application to join the club in a statement timed for the moribund week before the August bank holiday. The Commonwealth was not happy about losing access to British markets; there were some in the Tory Party who were not happy with the loss of sovereignty; the Labour Party was not happy about downgrading Britain's non-European international connections; the public was totally unprepared. Macmillan had been of necessity circumspect, but many were worried that he had not properly prepared the ground.

The French Superiority Complex

French President Charles de Gaulle was a unique phenomenon, a ghastly man who makes Jacques Chirac seem like a model of sweet reason. By the end of the Second World War, he had reinvented himself as not only the saviour, but the personification, of France, and seemed to regard the Anglo-Saxons (British and Americans) as the real enemy. He could sulk, lie, ill-treat his own supporters or turn a blind eye to torture by the French army and police (in Algeria). He saw WWII as a national affair, the re-establishment by France of its own government of which the restoration of European democracy was a minor collateral effect.

It is not quite true to say that he loathed Britain. Better to observe that he admired it, and saw it, like France, as an important player on the most important continent in the world. But, incapable of seeing anything in other than purely nationalist terms, that meant that Britain was *de facto* an enemy. In de Gaulle's oddly-shaped head, Euro-politics was a zero sum game; if someone else was up, France was down. And France and Britain had learned different lessons from Suez — the French would never again rely on the Americans, the British would never cross them.

Having inherited the EEC project upon becoming President in 1958, de Gaulle saw it as a counterbalance against the Atlanticist Anglo-Saxon powers. In his mind it was, in effect, a Greater France. It would work in French interests, pay for the inefficiencies of the French agricultural sector, and support France's international territories. Its industrial heartland on the Ruhr would boost French industry. It would project French interests on the international stage, where they belonged, in opposition to US and Soviet hegemony.

Whether or not de Gaulle ever considered the British application seriously, there is no doubt that the Gaullist view of the EEC would have been threatened by British entry. British agriculture was much more efficient after its pre-war rationalisation, and eventually would baulk at ladling endless quantities of moolah at less efficient peasant farmers. And no British government then or now would ever try to undermine America's superpower status.

But de Gaulle would need to be persuaded otherwise, because de Gaulle had a veto.

The Lord Privy Seal

When Macmillan decided to move Britain towards an application for membership in the Summer of 1960, he prepared the ground for a long haul of discussion, exploration and negotiation with a cabinet reshuffle. The key move, which altered the course of British history over the next fifteen years, was of the Chief Whip, Edward Heath, to the meaningless courtesy position of Lord Privy Seal. Heath was assigned special responsibility for matters European, and would deputise for Foreign Secretary Lord Home in the Commons.

Heath was of the great generation of Tory politicians elected in 1950, after the Labour landslide of 1945 had swept away the dead wood of the squires and blimps. A new group of Tories, younger, more energetic, and crucially (thanks to war service) with enough experience of a wide range of people to understand the problems of the nation of a whole rather than of a privileged class, had returned from the war to take their place; within this group, there was much jockeying for position to replace the prewar generation.

Heath, if not typical of the new wave, was certainly more typical of the country as a whole. A grammar school boy, he owed his position to brains and political skills, rather than parentage or wealth. As Chief Whip he had performed rather brilliantly, somehow holding the Tories together as a Parliamentary force during the Suez crisis and after, as well as engineering Macmillan's succession.

When one surveys the major politicians of the 1960s and 70s — as we shall have cause to do in Chapters Five and Six — the phenomenon that leaps to the eye is that they were all so very much larger than life, in contrast to today's grey managementspeaking clones. Heath was no exception. He was, it is true, a very dull, very stiff and very charmless man. But he was *so* dull, he became interesting by that very fact; he was *so* stiff that in his awkwardness he seemed one of us; he was *so* charmless that one couldn't help but nurture a sneaking soft spot for him. And yet at the same time there was a sort of cosmic aspect to him, as if he were the Platonic ideal of dull, stiff charmlessness.

His intellect was undoubted, and his energy was colossal; nowadays, energy is the premier requirement for a politician, but in the more relaxed 60s Heath stood out. His being unmarried seemed to symbolise much about him; he had no family to divert his energies, and his bachelor status chimed with his crustiness and coldness. Foreign affairs of the diplomatic kind were what really interested him, but, despite a maiden speech deploring the then Labour government's unimaginative response to the early stages of development of the future EEC institutions, Heath doesn't appear to have had a great deal of interest in the European project until round about Macmillan's conversion.

Other Cabinet changes put key Europhiles in important positions; Duncan Sandys took over Commonwealth Relations and Christopher Soames Agriculture (these two were Churchill's sons-in-law), each charged with the tricky task of squaring membership with potentially hostile interests. Sceptical players within the cabinet were cleverly neutralised. Macmillan's great rival Rab Butler, who was less appalled by Europe than unenthused by it, was placed in charge of the ministerial committee directing negotiations; Butler's careful, plodding and mild reformism probably held back progress, but ensured competence and one more positive voice within Cabinet. Heath's great rival Reggie Maudling, who had been instrumental in setting up EFTA, was shunted away from European policy.

A Thousand Years of History

On the Labour side of the house, there was relatively little sympathy for the European cause. There were, to be sure, some Euro-enthusiasts, George Brown, Anthony Crosland and Roy Jenkins among others, but their position cut little ice in a party riven by muscular shoving between left and right. They were in the inner circle of leader Hugh Gaitskell on the right of the party, but Gaitskell himself held a "so what?" position not unlike that of Rab Butler. Furthermore, he had only recently survived some very bruising encounters with the left of his party, having tried and failed to modernise its position on Clause 4 nationalisation and controlling the commanding heights of the economy, stood firm against unilateral nuclear disarmament and seen off a leadership challenge from Harold Wilson. Presumably he was hardly looking for another punch up.

Gaitskell tried to avoid any kind of a strong position, but as the membership application became a reality he found himself pushed to oppose it, partly on party political grounds, partly out of solidarity with the Commonwealth, and, one supposes, partly out of personal conviction. He did not relish the decision, particularly as it was an endorsement of his enemies' ideas made in the teeth of his friends' opposition. But he was a very able advocate of the anti position, most notably in his triumphant speech to the Labour Party conference in Brighton in 1962, in which he famously asserted that membership would involve sacrificing "a thousand years of island history".

It was one of the great political speeches, though his Deputy Leader George Brown, of whom more later, followed up Gaitskell's brilliant triumph with a clever, understated speech that, while not contradicting anything Gaitskell had said, left the door open for a future Labour *volte face*. Gaitskell had the last laugh, though. As leader of the opposition, likely, given the polls, to be the next Prime

Minister, the Common Market negotiators couldn't help but take his opposition into account.

Kangaroos

The talks, which began formally with Heath's presentation of the application in Paris in October 1961, were incredibly detailed. The important issues were the position of the Commonwealth with respect to the Community, the integration of the British into the Common Agricultural Policy (known as the CAP—the British, though they also provided artificial support for an uneconomic agricultural sector, had a different and arguably superior system), and of course the level of Britain's contribution to the budget. These actually don't sound too daunting in principle, and one possible option, urged by Jean Monnet among others, was that Britain could join the EEC quickly and in principle, and leaving the details to be thrashed out after joining. Monnet realised correctly that once in it would be hard to leave (actually, nothing in the Treaty of Rome allows for a country withdrawing from the EEC), whereas if all the details had to be worked out in advance, it would be infinitely harder to agree the conditions for entry. Better to move into an empty house and furnish it, than to insist on buying all the furniture in advance and hope the house is still for sale afterwards.

However, Monnet's suggestion was ignored, and as the Government's involvement in trade and industry was so much greater than we are used to now, that meant very tedious negotiations indeed. In her contemporary account of the arguments, Nora Beloff lists some of the commodities that had to be included separately and individually, with tariff levels set for each product of the Commonwealth countries: cricket bats, polo sticks, desiccated coconut, extract of mimosa. The six countries of the EEC worried about being swamped by British bacon and eggs unless British farmers were put immediately onto the European system of featherbedding farmers, rather than remaining for a transitional period on the British featherbed. Some agreements were straightforward: tariffs were abolished for Commonwealth-produced tinned kangaroo meat, for instance

Nor was the comprehensiveness of the negotiations the only problem. There were two obvious and sensible ways of conducting them. One would be a seven-way conference, with Britain and the Six sitting around the table together. Another, perfectly good, would be for bilateral talks between Britain and the European Commission. Given the choice between two sensible structures, need it be said that the Six chose a third, hopeless compromise? Britain would negotiate with the Six, who would act not as individual governments, but in concert as far as possible.

Under this diabolical system, for each and every item on the agenda, the Six would therefore have to conduct their own internal negotiations in order to thrash out a common position. That could be very time-consuming in itself. Then, given the common EEC position, they would then enter the negotiations proper with the British. In the event that the British demanded some movement or compromise, the Six would then have to disappear into a conclave again and reopen delicate issues that everyone hoped had been settled. This not only took terribly long periods of time, but also deterred compromise. It made Britain appear intransigent whenever a sticking point was reached. To cap it all, there was a rotating chairmanship, so that issues settled under one chairman were liable to be reopened under another.

Even that wasn't fiendish enough. To complicate things further, the Six themselves, even by the Autumn of 1961, had not yet finalised the details of their agreement. In particular, the final form of the CAP had not been settled. It would have been helpful, not only to the British, had the British been able to sit in on these separate negotiations and develop a policy that could cover a wider range of agricultural interests than the Six could envisage. Failing that, a quick conclusion to the membership negotiations would allow the British into the CAP talks as full members. But the French aim was to shape the CAP in their favour before worrying about how the British fitted in. It suited the French to drag out the membership negotiations to allow for the prior conclusion of the CAP talks between the Six.

Agreement on the CAP in early 1962 was followed by the Six's flat rejection of the British proposal to allow the Commonwealth favourable access to European markets. That suddenly increased the scope of the talks still further, as negotiations then had to deal with each country and each product separately, kangaroo meat and all.

The French continued to procrastinate even after the terms of the CAP were finalised, setting out a completely new set of proposals on temperate foodstuffs (whatever they may be) at the end of July 1962, and also demanding an impossible financial package for the British—all in the face of the opposition of their five supposed partners—in order to prevent the talks being completed provisionally before the August Summer break (which, for good measure, French

Foreign Minister Couve de Murville doubled in length, insisting on reconvening in October).

Given all this, Heath's conduct of the negotiations was masterful, his grasp of the detail extraordinary, his deployment of his hand-picked team deft. By January 1963, agreement had been reached on most matters, including tariff levels for 2,500 import products from the Commonwealth. Fewer than 30 product tariffs remained to be settled.

Pulling the Plug

But time was against Heath and the British. French Assembly elections strengthened de Gaulle's hand, while Macmillan's Government was faltering, and the anti-EEC Labour Party looked likely to become the next British government (as they duly did, in 1964). As public opinion moved against the Tories, it moved against the Common Market as well.

At the same time, Macmillan was getting to know President Kennedy in the US, which worried de Gaulle. When Kennedy cancelled the development of the Skybolt nuclear air-to-ground missile, which was behind schedule and over budget (like every defence project ever in the entire history of the world), Macmillan persuaded him to give the British access to Polaris missiles instead.

This merely convinced de Gaulle that Britain was primarily an Atlanticist power, not a European one. He might have changed his mind had the British agreed to share its more advanced nuclear technology with the French (who were desperate for it), but Macmillan made no such offer. And so, on the 14th January 1963 — when virtually all the major sticking points of the negotiations had been cleared — de Gaulle called a notorious press conference at the Elysée Palace, and exercised his veto against British membership. The General said "Non!"

He cited Britain's special habits and traditions, its incompatible trading system, its early scepticism of the European project. But the main reason was that Britain would be the thin end of a wedge; if Britain came in, a number of other countries would too, and the result would be an Atlantic community dominated, if not joined, by America.

The other five EEC nations were even more outraged than Britain; de Gaulle was isolated. Indeed, it wasn't even clear that the French negotiating team were aware of de Gaulle's intentions. Like a newly decapitated chicken, the negotiations carried on for a while, but once it became clear that de Gaulle was unmoveable and the veto would stay in place, the talks were called off on 29th January.

Four days later, Hugh Gaitskell died after a short and sudden illness; the leadership of the Labour Party, and soon afterwards the post of Prime Minister, fell into the lap of the left, in the shape of Harold Wilson. Heath's reputation, already good, was made by his conduct of the negotiations, despite their ending in failure. By 1965, he was the leader of his party.

Coda

This was not the last of Britain's doomed attempts to get into de Gaulle's Europe; a second attempt went off half-cocked in 1967. George Brown was another of those bizarre, larger-than-life 60s politicians. Short, jowly, argumentative, a brilliant populist on the right of the Labour Party, his greatest contribution to British politics was his fondness for alcohol, combined with a splendid ability to shake off tedious inhibitions under its influence. In these days of khaki Hoons and grey Hewitts, of family-friendly hours, of merciless press coverage of every deviation and peccadillo, it is impossible not to be nostalgic for the days when George Brown bestrode the world.

Brown was an outspoken pro-European, but he never let that get in the way of a good argument, even when he became Foreign Secretary. His biographer Peter Paterson tells the story of a discussion in the Quai d'Orsay when Brown suddenly began to abuse Valéry Giscard d'Estaing (future President of France, and later chairman of the EU constitutional convention). Giscard, whose English is fluent, understood every word, but Brown capped off his performance by telling a translator "You translate that for this Frog". On another occasion, at a banquet given by the Belgian government for Brown and his entourage, he only left after making the following contribution to international relations: "While you have been wining and dining here tonight, who has been defending Europe? I'll tell you who — the British army. And where, you may ask, are the soldiers of the Belgian Army tonight? They're in the brothels of Brussels."

On the topic of Europe, Harold Wilson's views were not dissimilar to Gaitskell's; initially, he didn't really care. As something of an internationalist, he was more interested in the Commonwealth and the problems of the developing world. However, by 1966 the Labour Party was becoming more interested in the EEC. Relations with the Commonwealth were souring, and the economy was a disaster area, thanks to a misguided policy to keep a strong pound. So — as in

1961 – getting Britain into Europe began to look like a fresh policy initiative after a bad period for the Government.

Wilson does not seem to have made Brown Foreign Secretary in 1966 in order to promote the European cause, but that was the net result. Brown presented Wilson with a series of reports about European relations in the Autumn, which seem to have persuaded him. Eventually, despite some divisions, Wilson got the Cabinet's agreement by majority (although some anti-marketeers, like Richard Crossman, acquiesced in the application confident that de Gaulle would veto it again).

To prepare the ground, Wilson and Brown decided on the odd course of making flying visits, in early 1967, to all Six nations of the EEC to meet their premiers and foreign ministers. Inevitably with Brown on board, one or two of the welcoming banquets and beanfeasts got out of hand, but no-one declared war, so that was alright.

The surprise effect was on Wilson. Lukewarm to begin with, accepting the case for entry with his head but not his heart, the requirements of diplomatic advocacy seem to have energised him, so that he became almost as committed as Brown. His main mission, as was obvious after the debacle of 1963, was to persuade de Gaulle. What he actually did, ironically, was persuade himself.

Did he persuade de Gaulle? Not in the least. Lanky de Gaulle received his two diminutive visitors with politeness, and listened to their pitch. He responded with faint praise, recognising the distance that the British, and the Labour Party in particular, had moved, but adding only that that was an encouraging sign. He suggested a couple of ways that Britain could be associated with the EEC without actually being a member thereof.

Wilson was too fired up to take the hint and, with the backing of his fractious Parliamentary party and the Cabinet, announced his application on 2nd May 1967. It took de Gaulle two whole weeks to reject the doomed proposal. On his analysis, only three options were possible. First, the EEC could be destroyed and a new one built by the Six, Britain, and any others who were interested (he added that this would merely be the precursor to an Atlantic free trade zone that would take away Europe's personality). Second, Britain (and the other EFTA countries) could be associates of the EEC. Or third, everyone could "wait for the change to be brought about by the internal and external developments of which, it seems, England [sic] is showing signs."

In still other words, "Non, toujours!" De Gaulle waited until November to deliver the inevitable official veto. But that was the moment when George Brown's clever political instincts overcame the buffoon in him. At a difficult Cabinet meeting (the veto had coincided with yet another run on sterling, a humiliating devaluation and a Cabinet reshuffle), where the majority opinion was one of relief that the veto had got the Labour government out of a pickle, Brown carried his argument that the application should stay on the table, for a future government to revive after de Gaulle had left the scene.

Chapter Two
Ted Takes Us In — Will Harold Bring Us Out?

A New Opportunity

After two failures, the British might have flounced off in a huff; actually, so dismal was British economic performance compared to the Europeans' that "joining Europe" was still seen by many to be the key to progress. Access to those big juicy markets remained a driving force for a small number of zealous thinkers.

Heath was easily the more pro-European of the two party leaders. Wilson was constitutionally-inclined to see both sides of a question, and tended to adopt more nuanced stances. Furthermore at that stage of British history, it was Wilson's Labour Party that was the more fissile and hard to manage. On the other hand, it was Wilson who had the 100-plus majority in Parliament.

It was clear with hindsight that the chief obstacle to British entry was de Gaulle. Though the EEC was not his creation, he had done much to turn it into an instrument of French foreign policy. The West Germans were prepared, for political and historical reasons, to play a secondary role to the French in running the Community, but de Gaulle was under no illusions that Britain, as another similarly-sized player, would also take a back seat — and Britain's diplomatic outlook (Atlanticist), economic structure (outward-looking based on trade) and philosophical nature (empiricist and pragmatic) were so different from France's that it was unlikely that the two countries could pull together in the same direction.

So the conventional expressions of sympathy that accompanied de Gaulle's resignation in April 1969 — ironically, after failure to win a referendum — were perhaps a tad less sincere than usual. Wilson's Government immediately began to prepare the ground for a third attempt to join, even as de Gaulle's successor Georges Pompidou made more positive noises (the remaining Five, meanwhile, continued to press for British entry). Wilson called an election he was bound to win for June 1970, and negotiations would begin, under George Thomson, once that formality was out of the way.

There's many a slip ... Against almost all the polls, Labour lost the election, and the Tories were returned with a majority of 30. Heath's manifesto was certainly pro-European, but made no mention of actually joining ("Our sole commitment is to negotiate; no more, no less"). The Common Market was barely mentioned in the campaign, but Europe did play a strange part: the country seemed to be plunged into pessimism in the week before the election when England were beaten in the World Cup at the quarter final stage, 3–2 by West Germany, after leading 2–0. Poor old George Brown lost his seat in the carnage.

A question remained: with the Tories and the Liberals very much for, and the Labour Party lukewarm but also in favour, there had been little public debate. Did that legitimise opening serious negotiations?

More Negotiations

Given Heath's biggest ambition was to take Britain into the EEC, it is doubtful that he even considered that question. Negotiations began in Luxembourg before the end of June.

Wilson's failure to learn the lessons of 1963 doomed his own attempt from the beginning. Heath made no such mistake. French opposition (even under Pompidou) to British entry was the most serious obstacle. Macmillan's strategy had been to use the pro-British Five to shift the French on his behalf, but 1963 had shown that the Five, even in concert, could not move the French far enough. The only way for Britain to join would be to negotiate directly with, and so persuade, the French. The French had to buy into the deal; they would not bow to the majority view. A veto was a veto.

Negotiations began properly in October, the British team led by Geoffrey Rippon, and ran much more smoothly. The British (both politicians and civil servants) now knew so much more about how the Common Market did its business that many dead ends were avoided. And it should not be forgotten that in 1970 the EEC was twice as old as it had been in 1962; even its own members knew correspondingly more about how it worked. On top of that, the negotiations took place at a higher level, and were therefore clearer of detail; kangaroo meat and bacon didn't feature this time. And now the President of the Council of Ministers spoke for all of the Six, so negotiations carried on between two bodies rather than an unwieldy seven.

France stalled on the British contribution to the budget, and sterling's role as a world currency, although it wasn't clear whether it was merely driving a hard bargain or trying to wreck the talks to avoid having to apply the veto a third time. Presumably it was keeping its options open between the two. On the budget, the French wanted the British to pay 21% of the EEC budget with no transition period. This was a hard demand, of which the French would be the chief beneficiaries, but the British were in a tough spot; the French had made it a condition of negotiation that the CAP remain in place as it was. And since the British wanted to join more than the French wanted them to, Rippon's position was weak.

With respect to sterling's role, it was accepted on all sides that its status as a world currency had to go if monetary union were to be achieved by the end of the decade, the stated aim of the Commission. The British were not averse to sterling becoming less of a crux in the world economy, because in those times of exchange rate micromanagement, maintaining a particular rate was made harder by international movements of capital. But equally everyone realised that downgrading sterling from an international currency would take time and patient work. Overseas holdings of sterling would have to be run down gradually.

Hence the pound was officially excluded from the talks. At which point, the ever-helpful French launched an attack on sterling's world role, demanding that it be curtailed immediately if the talks were to succeed. It began to seem that Pompidou was prepared to use his veto after all — or let Britain in only on impossibly stringent conditions.

The slow progress of these negotiations in Spring 1971 helped the anti-market forces to rally. Almost half Labour's MPs signed a Commons motion against entry, and their Tory counterparts were marshalling their arguments too. Characteristically, Wilson began to shift his position; he did not oppose entry, but hinted that he would oppose the terms that Rippon negotiated. The public became hostile; 70% opposed entry.

But Sir Christopher Soames, British ambassador to France, was working behind the scenes, and secured crucial French movement in May. The British contribution to the EEC budget was agreed in outline, beginning at 8.6% and moving to 19% five years after joining. The sterling question was thrashed out by Heath and Pompidou personally in a summit meeting; the two of them, meeting for the first time, got on well. The French accepted the British position on sterling, and all the other supposed disagreements of principle melted away with Pompidou's hostility. Heath was able to publish a white paper setting out the terms of entry in early July, 1971.

The "Great Debate"

The white paper was supposed to promote what Heath called the "Great Debate", intended to shift public and political opinion round to the EEC, using the momentum gained by the successful conclusion of the negotiations and the agreement on terms to promote the EEC cause. A huge government publicity campaign was launched, beginning with a glossy brochure published on the same day as the white paper. Heath must have thought he was home and dry.

Sadly, he wasn't. In the country, opinion steadfastly refused to move away from rejectionism. In Parliament the large pro-EEC majority was waning as Labour shifted against membership and the Tory malcontents developed a coherent critique based on the loss of sovereignty. Joining the EEC would mean that, for the first time, British law could be changed by agents outside the UK, unbeholden to British voters. Heath's counter-argument was that Britain's greatness in the world demanded that it joined the EEC. Why this was wasn't made entirely clear.

Alongside this stuff of high principle, there was a noisy buzz of argument about whether or not prices would rise, or working patterns change, and so on. So boring was all this that no-one really listened.

Labour wasn't all that keen on the Great Debate. Wilson had cooled again, and in opposition was keener to score political points off Heath (which he could do all day — Wilson's quick intelligence unanchored to principle trounced Heath's wooden stolidity over and again in the ten years they faced each other). George Brown's successor as Deputy Leader, Roy Jenkins, was very pro-Europe. But the majority of his party was now turning against. Wilson's great skill was keeping Labour united; the way to do that, with strong and vocal elements both pro- and anti-EEC, was to get everyone to rally around an attack on the Tories' terms of entry. This compromise allowed Labour's U-turn to be disguised; their position could be represented as being in favour in principle, though against the actual terms. Much of the opposition, though, was rooted in a principled objection to joining a capitalist club (as Soames had not too helpfully called it); a number of Labour MPs at this time might well have preferred membership of the Warsaw Pact. They weren't opposed to high taxes *per se*, but they certainly didn't want the proceeds to go to French farmers.

The Parliamentary Vote

The key moment was a Parliamentary vote scheduled for the Autumn on whether to accept the white paper's terms. Heath had made an unfortunate commitment that Britain should not join without "full-hearted" consent of Parliament and people, and so a thumping majority would be handy.

But the shifting patterns of loyalty demanded clever tactics. Should the Government put a whip on the debate? If they did, Labour would then whip their MPs in turn, so the vote would be totally party political. The Tories had 330 MPs, Labour 287, and with 13 others 316 were needed for a majority. But each side had rebels. Labour had more MPs unhappy with the party line, but the mood was dark and a whip would probably be enough to keep the pro-Europe Labour MPs out of the Government lobby; relatively few Labour MPs were prepared to go to the wall for Heath's glory, particularly as they could always salve their conscience by pleading unhappiness with the terms of entry. On the other hand, the Tory rebels were getting increasingly cross and insistent that Heath had no mandate for what he was doing. Though the Tory antis were smaller in number than the Labour pros, they were more likely to rebel.

So a whipped vote wouldn't produce a large majority; indeed, it was not certain to produce a majority at all. And one of the rebels' contentions was that a slim margin on a whipped vote did not constitute full-hearted consent by Parliament. So—on their fevered reasoning—Heath's own condition for joining would not be met, and so we shouldn't join. Of course, no-one seriously considered that Heath would accept such a calculation himself, but it was an agreeable stick to beat him with.

Chief Whip Francis Pym argued strongly for a free vote. Whipping would make little difference to the rebels; most would defy it anyway. On the other side of the house, though, Labour's splits were so deep that a free vote would help the pro-European cause. Whereas few Labour MPs would defy a whip to vote 'no', they would be much more likely to vote 'yes' if it didn't "officially" involve voting with the government. In which case, because of the larger number of Labour rebels a free vote would produce a bigger majority for membership. The unofficial organiser of Labour's pro-Europeans, William Rodgers, lobbied Heath hard for a free vote.

But Heath's pride was at least as strongly engaged as his brain. Joining the EEC was probably the only major policy that Heath didn't reverse, and he considered it essential to get this flagship measure through the house without relying on Labour votes, so he remained very attached to the idea of whipping his MPs through the 'yes' lobby. In the end, good sense won out. Pym, Rippon, Willie Whitelaw, Tony Barber and Lord Carrington sat on Heath in a small room in the House of Commons and pulled his hair until he agreed a free vote for the Tory MPs.

All the calculations were that Labour would follow suit. But now enters our story another of its heroes, Tony Benn. Benn, a pro-European in 1962 and 1967, had switched sides with the zeal of the convert, and furthermore had begun his one-man campaign to turn Britain into a socialist republic. With the tactical ineptitude that characterised the Benn revolution he insisted that the Labour whip stayed on, and Wilson acquiesced.

Benn wanted to make life hard for the pro-Europeans, but probably not for the first time, certainly not for the last, he handed victory to the Tories. Heath, ironically, got all the credit for allowing the House of Commons to express its own will; Wilson looked, in contrast, like a petty party politician. As Pym had calculated, the free vote made little difference to the Tory rebels, but the Labour rebels were emboldened to vote against their party whip because they could not be accused (or, rather, they could be accused but they could take no notice) of supporting the Government.

The end was a triumph for Heath: 356–244, a majority of 112. 69 Labour MPs rebelled, 20 abstaining, while 39 Tories voted against the motion (not strictly a rebellion because of the free vote), 2 abstaining. The Lords, on a similar motion, supported it by 451–58. Parliament's will seemed clear.

Who Governs Britain? Not You, Ted

There were relatively few triumphs for Heath during his unhappy period of office; it is beyond question that the successful bid for EEC membership was the largest. Ted was a disastrous Prime Minister. Industrial problems derailed his government almost from the start. The trade unions, unpopular yet irresistible, turned on Heath, and his Industrial Relations Act. The miners took the lead, but Heath was beset with strikes all round. In 1973, the oil shock hit, and further unrest down the mines in early 1974 prompted Heath to bring in the three-day week—incredible to imagine now, but such were the shortages of energy and other materials that rationing was brought in and the working week halved. People huddled round hoarded candles. Right wingers were affronted by Heath's reneging on the free market policies on which he had been elected (he nationalised Rolls-Royce and Upper Clyde Shipbuilders, and implemented a pay freeze after promising to avoid statutory pay policy). Meanwhile, Northern Ireland exploded into violence.

As his authority ebbed, the EEC rebels were getting organised, and the complex enabling legislation required for membership got a rough ride, particularly as the Labour pro-Europeans, having made their principled stand, had resumed party political business as usual. The majority slipped, on occasion, to single figures. As it was, the legislation passed, just, and Britain joined the EEC on 1st January 1973, together with Ireland and Denmark. The highlight of the celebrations was a representative football match at Wembley on the 3rd in which The Three, managed by England manager Sir Alf Ramsay and controversially stuffed with English players, beat The Six 2–0—with goals by two non-Englishmen.

After that high spot it was downhill all the way for both Europe and Ted. The EEC got some of the blame for the economic problems that followed membership, in particular the rampant inflation. On top of that, the "British Banger Replaced By Eurosausage" scare stories that still turn up on quiet days in the madder British tabloids began to appear.

Meanwhile, Heath had domestic problems too. The miners' strike in early 1974 prompted him to call an early election on the theme of "Who governs Britain?" He was expected to win, although a close call was predicted; Wilson was not popular either, and both had been peculiarly bad Prime Ministers.

The most startling intervention came just before the election; Enoch Powell quit as a Tory Parliamentary candidate on the day the election was announced, and followed this with a pair of blistering speeches in which he urged people to vote Labour, on the ground that EEC membership was the most important issue facing the nation. Whereas continuing membership was a certainty with the Tories, at least there was a chance of withdrawal under Labour.

The second of these speeches, at Shipley in Yorkshire as part of a 'Get Britain Out' rally, was one of the great pieces of British political theatre. As Powell developed an extraordinary attack on Heath, a heckler shouted "Judas!" Powell fixed him with a beady eye and replied, with not a great deal of hesitation: "Judas was paid! Judas was paid! I am making a sacrifice!" The treachery ended Powell's hopes of ever leading the Tory Party, and Heath's of winning the election. Which was Holmes and which Moriarty as they plunged together off the Reichenbach Falls depends, I suppose, on one's point of view.

The election, between two tired, weak leaders, was an effective tie; the Tories got marginally more votes, Labour marginally more seats, but no Parliamentary majority. Wilson ran a minority administration, called a second election in October on the back of expectations of an easy win — and gained a majority of just 3.

The sequel was Ted's defenestration. Heath, having lost three elections out of four to Wilson, having lost the confidence of many in his party, and not having the charm to get round the difficulty, was challenged to a leadership election by Margaret Thatcher, at that time famous only for being the former Education Secretary who banned free school milk. To everyone's surprise, not least Ted's, Thatcher prevailed. On 11th February 1975, the Tories had a new leader, lukewarmly pro-European.

Renegotiation

Labour's manifesto for February 1974 was still not opposed to membership in principle, although its activists were increasingly restive. The only way to square the circle was a tough renegotiation. Those with strong opinions on Europe — Jenkins, Harold Lever, Shirley Williams (all for), Benn, Michael Foot and Barbara Castle (against) were given Cabinet positions to keep them away from the negotiations. The key position of Foreign Secretary went to Jim Callaghan, like Wilson sceptical but uncommitted. The renegotiations saved everyone's face; the pro-Europeans could sound anti-Tory, the antis could will the renegotiations to fail.

Callaghan began with a blunt speech in April 1974, which provoked hostile comment from the other members, but he ruled out renegotiating the Treaty of Rome or the Treaty of Accession which had brought Britain in. The day after Callaghan's speech, the ailing Pompidou died; naturally everything stopped until a new French President, Giscard d'Estaing, was in place. Giscard, despite having been on the receiving end of George Brown some years before, was somewhat better disposed to British demands than his two predecessors.

When negotiations reconvened in June, the Labour ministers (both those involved in the negotiations and those not) were rather happier with the EEC, having seen it in action and dealt with it on a practical level. Callaghan was notably more conciliatory. The tone shifted; in April, the aim of the negotiations was to meet British needs on pain of the British blocking the EEC's work, whereas by June there was a more businesslike approach on both sides. The EEC played a vanishingly small part once again in the October 1974 election campaign, but after Labour's marginal victory, everything was back on track.

The negotiations finally ground to a halt in March 1975, with a renegotiated package little different from the original terms. Wilson recommended the new deal to the British people. His achievement was a postponement of his decision for a year. That was, of course, no small thing — indeed, it is the reason that Britain is still a member of the EU thirty years later. Had it not taken place, and Wilson had to make a snap decision in March 1974, the chances of Britain pulling out would have been a lot higher.

But with a renegotiated package, it was now time to consult the people.

Hey ... Let's Consult The People Right Here!

Why the people? After all, hadn't there just been two general elections? Wasn't there a perfectly legitimate Parliament in place? Wasn't it the role of the people's elected representatives to make these complex decisions? Isn't that what representative democracy is?

The referendum crept up slowly and silently; it had become Labour Party policy almost accidentally, in 1972. As the European Communities Bill was running through Parliament, it crashed into one of Enoch Powell's ambushes — an amendment demanding a consultative referendum before Britain could join the EEC.

Parenthetically we should note the inconsistency on Powell's part, as Enoch was always very keen to excoriate Heath for similar "tergiversation". In the 1970 election campaign, Powell had explicitly claimed to be "no supporter of a referendum." Of the many reasons he said he had for this view, he rehearsed two, of which the second, that without knowing the terms one couldn't vote in an informed way, had been superseded by the successful conclusion of Rippon's negotiations. But the first reason, that it is inconsistent with the responsibility of government to Parliament and to the electorate, remained valid. A U-turn of his own? What had changed? Well, obviously he thought that his view would prevail in a referendum, with public opinion as it was.

Tony Benn had originally raised the referendum idea in a meeting of the National Executive Committee of the Labour Party in 1970, but had had no takers. In 1972 he tried again, proposing it to the Shadow Cabinet while the Powell amendment was before Parliament. Again, no takers. A week later, though, the NEC passed the measure by 13-11. A week after that, the Shadow Cabinet supported the referendum idea by 8-6, and it became Labour Party policy.

Skullduggery was suspected. Indeed, Jenkins resigned as Deputy Leader and from the Shadow Cabinet, warning darkly that "by this means [i.e. introducing a referendum] we would have forged a more powerful weapon against progressive legislation than anything we have known in this country since the curbing of the absolute powers of the House of Lords." Glad to see the back of him, the Parliamentary Labour Party endorsed the Shadow Cabinet decision, and in the end most voted for the Powell amendment—which was defeated anyway.

Why the sudden change? There seem to be three reasons. First, there was the prospect of party political joy from defeating Heath on something, anything. Second, the referendum was clearly a device for the anti-marketeers, who guessed from the opinion polls that the referendum would produce a 'no' vote.

Third, it gave the leadership a way out of a nasty spot. The upper echelons of the Labour Party contained fanatical pros and fanatical antis, and Wilson knew what could happen to a party when this happened on an issue—the Gaitskell-Bevan struggle throughout the 1950s had handed power to the Tories for a generation.

If Wilson had failed to win the 1974 elections, then he could have ranted and raged to his heart's content without making any decisions at all. But he did win. Renegotiation was the next stalling procedure. But renegotiation would eventually finish, which it did. That left a package, which Wilson either had to implement or not, and when that decision was made, he would alienate half his party. But a referendum laid the onus on the voters themselves. Whatever happened, Wilson could say to whichever faction was affronted "Had it been up to me, I would have gone along with you. But the people have spoken. My hands are tied."

Maybe all great constitutional changes are made because of such calculations. Maybe.

Chapter Three
Referendums, Practice and Theory

How Did We Get Here?

OK, that's a lot of narrative. The history of European Union, as a serious, boring project undertaken by bureaucrats (i.e. the sort of project that might actually succeed), as opposed to a flamboyant, showy project undertaken by generals (the sort which won't), covers about sixty years; Britain's euro-referendum occurred exactly at the half-way point.

Labour came round to the referendum idea as a neat device, partly to help Wilson keep the Labour Party together, and partly as a means to discomfit Heath during the passage of the European Communities Bill. As it was, it failed in the latter aim, though it succeeded in the former — at least in the short term.

Heath and Jenkins were against a referendum, Benn and Powell for. All of these, bar Heath, were keen historians (Jenkins wrote many books of history, Powell two or three) and experts on the constitution. Heath, though not a scholar, as a former Chief Whip knew as much about the practicalia of Parliamentary business as anyone. These four, brilliantly intelligent all, could work out whether a referendum was compatible with Britain's unwritten constitution of representative democracy. Yet — how strange! — they failed to reach a consensus about it. And — stranger still! — their opinions diverged in the same way as their divide over Europe. The pro-Europeans were anti-referendum, anti-Europeans pro-referendum. What gives? Was it simply because, with the EEC unpopular in the opinion polls, the anti-Europeans thought that they could win the referendum, and the pro-Europeans thought that they would lose? Can it really be that our finest constitutional practitioners gave no thought for the proprieties and precedents, and pondered the whole issue from the perspective of whether their preferred policy would end up on the statute book?

Yes it can (although to be fair to Tony Benn, his interest in direct democracy began before the EEC issue, and he did advocate a referendum on the EEC long before anyone else; Enoch Powell, as we have seen, strongly opposed a referendum in 1970). The adoption of the referendum—contingent on so many things, including Heath's misguided call for a general election in February 1974, the position of the Labour Party in the late 60s and early 70s, and, if Roy Jenkins' memoirs are to be believed, the fact that Ted Short turned up late for the fateful Shadow Cabinet meeting in March 1972—happened, and might not have happened, for reasons that have nothing to do with its desirability, or its effectiveness, or its correctness.

The referendum happened because of the accidental circumstance that the people who thought that they could win it had superior control of the institutions of power at the right time. Not, one has to say, a good reason. Can we find a better one?

The Precedents

The referendum that took place in 1975 on EEC membership was actually the first and so far only national referendum in Britain, so in a strict sense there were no precedents. However, the possibility of referendums had been canvassed before to resolve impasses in British politics, usually by Tories, usually as a way of avoiding rapid social change.

Referendums had most often been proposed to deal with the problems of Ireland and Northern Ireland, because those were the geographical areas where the legitimacy of rule from Westminster and the active consent of the people ruled were most problematic. A.V. Dicey, a famous constitutional scholar of the late 19th century, wanted a national vote throughout the United Kingdom on the question of home rule for Ireland (the question that tore Gladstone's Liberal Party apart in the 1890s), on the assumption that the national vote would be against it. When the issue flared up again just before the First World War, once again a referendum was mooted as a way of working out which bits of Ireland, if any, should be handed over to a putative Dublin government.

And when a major referendum *was* held for the first time on British soil, it was in Northern Ireland in 1973 following the rise in violence that caused the suspension of the Northern Irish government at Stormont. No doubt that exercise, on the question of whether

Northern Ireland should remain part of the United Kingdom, influenced Wilson. Whether it was a *good* precedent is another question; the vote was boycotted by Catholics while Protestants voted in huge numbers, delivering an unrepresentative result of 98.9% in favour, on a decent-sounding turnout of 58.7%. Again, what the 1973 referendum showed is that, unanchored by a political culture that values regular direct consultation of the people, consent to the consultative principle will depend largely on whether one thinks one can win. The Ulster Catholics, knowing that they were in a minority in the province, refused to vote in order not to legitimise a consultation process that was bound to result in defeat for their view.

There had also been sporadic attempts to suggest referendums to decide national issues, away from the fraught and *sui generis* politics of Ulster. The constitutional crisis of 1910, when the House of Lords rejected Lloyd George's budget, led the Tories to suggest that impasses between the Lords and the Commons might be resolved via referendums. As A.J. Balfour put it in his election address, "If you ask me whether this constitutional machinery could not be improved, either by some change in the composition of the House of Lords, or by the institution of a Referendum, I am certainly not going even to suggest a negative reply." Winston Churchill twice suggested referendums, in 1920 to resolve the question of votes for women, and again in 1945 to decide whether the British government, elected in 1935, should continue after the victory in the European theatre of the Second World War until the defeat of Japan (Labour leader Clement Attlee turned the offer down, and won the ensuing general election by a landslide, though whether either man's attitude towards a referendum was conditioned by his expectations of the election result isn't clear). In the 1930s, it was mooted that food taxes might be put to referendum.

There had been a number of minor, local referendums, on not-worth-the-bother questions such as whether cinemas or Welsh pubs should open on Sundays, or whether free public libraries should be established. But at a national level, no proposal had ever been enshrined even in draft legislation.

Initiatives for national or large regional referendums always seemed to stem from Tories or Liberals, or, in the case of Churchill, both. Referendums were seen as a way of mobilising the "common sense" of the British people against radical reformers' Utopian socialistic dreams. Conversely, the Labour Party generally opposed them for more or less the same reason. A Fabian tract by Clifford D.

Sharp in 1911, *The Case Against the Referendum*, makes a representative argument, echoed unconsciously in Roy Jenkins' resignation letter of 1972.

It can't be argued that direct democracy had had a glorious history in Britain on which the constitutional reformers of 1975 could draw.

Abroad

The referendum has been a popular tool in a number of other countries. It is often argued (based on the evidence of Hitler and Mussolini)[1] that the referendum is a useful tool for dictators to manipulate public opinion and to gain legitimacy for controversial measures. This, even if true, is of course a spectacular *non sequitur*, as not even his worst enemy would call Harold Wilson, who spent most of his political career, as he picturesquely phrased it, wading through shit to keep his party together, an evil dictator. Well, no-one except Lord Hailsham in his 1976 Dimbleby Lecture, whose worry about elective dictatorships miraculously disappeared when he became Lord Chancellor in a much sterner government than ever Wilson could sustain.

If we look at European democracies in the period 1900–1975, then the number of referendums that took place in that period isn't huge (Switzerland, the exception, is discussed a little later). Table 1 lists some prominent ones. Some of them are relevant here: Ireland, Denmark and Norway all applied to join the EEC simultaneously with Britain, although Norway surprisingly voted against membership in a crotchety affair. And at the same time, the French held a referendum to legitimise the idea of expanding the community (ironically, it is now musing over a referendum to *prevent* the community from expanding, by keeping Turkey out). These results are summarised in Table 2; as can be seen, the turnouts are respectable and the votes, pro and anti, clear cut. Ironically not a single one of the six signatories to the Treaty of Rome in 1957 put the decision to referendum.

---

[1] Hitler ran four referendums, each of which went his way with huge majorities on huge turnouts, between 1933 and 1938. These are obviously not included in Table 1 as Nazi Germany doesn't quite qualify as a democracy. Mussolini ran two others, again each of which were won comfortably. A referendum in 1934 approved his fascist regime by 99.9% to 0.1%, on a turnout of 99.5%, which just goes to show how much people appreciated trains running on time. Mr Blair and Railtrack take note.

Table 1: Number of Referendums in Selected European Democracies 1900–1975[2]

Country	No.	Country	No.	Country	No.
Belgium	1	Greece	4	Norway	5
Denmark	13	Iceland	4	Sweden	3
Finland	1	*Ireland*	7	*Switzerland*	204
France	10	Italy	2	Turkey	1
Germany	2	Luxembourg	3		

Table 2: Referendums with Respect to the Second Wave of Countries Joining the EEC

Country	Date	Issue	Turnout	Yes vote
France	23rd April, 1972	Expansion of the EEC	60.7%	67.7%
Ireland	10th May, 1972	Joining EEC	70.9%	83.1%
Norway	24th-25th Sept, 1972	Joining EEC	77.6%	46.5%
Denmark	2nd Oct, 1972	Joining EEC	90.1%	63.3%

Most of the non-Swiss referendums counted in Table 1 were on constitutional issues, such as approving a new constitution, amending an existing one, or changing minor arrangements (Denmark between 1939 and 1971 voted 5 times on lowering its voting age). A few were about territorial issues, France gave Algeria self-determination in 1961 and Iceland joined a union with Denmark in 1918. A few moral issues have been exposed to the glare of a referendum campaign, typically hot potatoes like alcohol, divorce and the like.

There are countries that are much more enthusiastic about referendums, notably the super-democracies of the United States and Switzerland. The US is founded on democratic principles in deliberate contrast to the European monarchies its founders wished to escape. The Swiss are a relatively diverse people living in a number of natural fortresses: robust federalist political institutions, direct democracy and subsidiarity are absolute requirements to keep such a nation together. The average Swiss has the opportunity to vote every few weeks on issues ranging from working out routes for new

---

[2] Countries in italics have mandatory referendum provisions in their constitutions. Source: Butler & Ranney, *Referendums*, pp. 11–13, 52–62.

roads to abolishing the army (a measure they rejected by a 3-1 majority in 2001). Turnouts in both countries are pretty low.

But it is not clear that Switzerland or the US are reasonable models for Britain to follow. The constitutions of both countries are designed to incorporate frequent referendums, and the decisions that issue from them; in each nation, there is a linear line of development from open town meetings to the referendums of today. In such systems, it would be an unacceptable centralisation of power if the political elites monopolised the determination of the questions that could be put to the people, and as one might expect both countries allow citizen initiatives; in Switzerland 100,000 signatures are required, collected over 18 months, to trigger a national referendum on an issue. 50,000 signatures in 100 days get you a referendum on a new law or amendment to an existing law.

There is a British film from 1970 called *The Rise and Rise of Michael Rimmer*, starring Peter Cook as the eponymous PR man who becomes President of Britain by monitoring public opinion and dictating politicians' reactions to it. In the end, as Prime Minister, he subjects the British to so many referendums that they get incredibly bored with the whole process and make Rimmer President for life—in a referendum!

Rimmer, who is scarily like Tony Blair, ever-smiling, ever ready with the right thing to say at the right time, understands the nature of the political system in Britain. We have an intellectual division of labour, which means that we can take little interest in politics if we so desire while specialists evaluate the arguments and take the decisions. Our representatives take decisions on our behalf, and more or less in accordance with our opinions, though they are emphatically not obliged to act on those opinions if they are persuaded otherwise. This representative theory was perhaps best stated by John Stuart Mill, in his *Considerations on Representative Government*. In a system run on those lines, the use of a referendum, uncontroversial in those nations like Switzerland and the US with a long tradition of direct democracy, requires a change in the citizen's role. And maybe, as *Michael Rimmer* implicitly suggests, such a change could lead to problems.

Well, having brought theory into it, what are the theories for and against referendums? How do they stack up?

Theory: The Case for Referendums

The case for referendums is effectively twofold, being based around the linked concepts of participation and legitimation. The idea of participation counters the fear that professional politicians, even democratic ones, can get out of touch with their constituents. People need to be politically engaged if they are to hold their representatives to proper account. They can't just abrogate all responsibility — or if they do, they can't complain when said representatives make stupid decisions, or squirrel the defence budget away in a Swiss bank account. And a referendum, where people have to, in effect, make the decision themselves, debate the questions, read the literature, watch the news, take part in discussions, and then decide without the comfort of intermediaries, precisely involves taking responsibility.

In very direct democracies, responsibility is taken seriously. In Ancient Athens, for example, members of the *polis* spent a lot of time engaged in the political questions of the day, and the Greek city-state system only began to break down when politics and related matters such as military affairs, began to be professionalised and specialised. Similarly, the Swiss, by and large, value their right to vote. The Americans, appallingly ignorant about the world at large, are often surprisingly well-informed about their own politics, at local, state and national level.

Establishing legitimacy is the other major reason for referendums. Legitimacy, on the theory of political scientist David Beetham, rests on three pillars. First, the actions of the state need to be in accordance with its own laws. Second, the laws themselves need to be justifiable to the population at large. Third, that justification has to be seen to have been successfully made by the people demonstrating their consent in some way or other (in a democracy, the most obvious way to do this is by voting). In an age where popular sovereignty is by far the most commonly accepted source of legitimacy, this last pillar is increasingly important, and it is therefore worrying for the authorities that turnouts seem to be in decline.

So the theory goes that decisions by referendum are more legitimate than those made by intermediaries or representatives, because the people not only show their consent, but they actually make the law themselves. Furthermore, since the second pillar of legitimacy involves the justifiability of the laws themselves, there is, on this reading, an even stronger justification for a referendum on the most fundamental laws, most obviously those enshrined in a constitution. Of course, the legitimacy of the decision depends on the turnout for the referendum, and the level of participation in the debate.

This is a good, serious positive argument for a referendum on the EEC issue in 1975, because in the European Communities Act Parliament had voted to deprive itself of certain unspecified and unspecifiable powers at some indeterminate time in the future. This was quite clearly a fundamental alteration to the British constitution.

Theory: The Case Against Referendums

On the other hand, there is a strong case against referendums as well. First, they weaken elected representatives and the system of representation. Our representatives can't govern properly if they think that the electorate is breathing down their necks. If representatives think that they might be kicked out of office for making the unpopular choice, then, although that may be healthy in some circumstances, it may well be very unhealthy in others. For instance, a representative who ignored the interests of his constituents regularly, or on some key issue, should expect to be booted out of office. But equally important political facts reach wide audiences only through imperfect intermediaries. Responsible and civilised politicians often find themselves marginalised if they try to suggest that the world might be a tad more complex than the buffoons of the press and the populist parties would have us believe. These are precisely the moments where it helps to encapsulate decision-makers; otherwise we would have hanging, flogging, the Dangerous Dogs Act, zero immigration, compulsory repatriation and petrol at 50p a gallon. As it is, we only have the Dangerous Dogs Act.

Actually, this argument can be turned on its head to make a similar conclusion. We elect our representatives; we pay them a lot of dosh (actually not that much compared with similarly stressful jobs, but that's a different matter). We pay them to weigh up the evidence, and we also pay them to be brave enough to argue the case when they are convinced, whether it be for a carbon tax, or road pricing, or legalising recreational drugs, or invading a large Middle Eastern country on a spurious pretext—or joining the EEC—however unpopular the policy may be. If they fail to make the case, then they may of course be turfed out by the electorate, but that is a risk they take if they do what they believe to be the right thing. And we pay them to take that risk; that is part of the job. To argue that politicians must *follow* public opinion, measured through focus groups or whatever, and do what the public (or, rather, that tiny section of the public that lives in key marginal seats) wants, is like arguing that a steeplejack should be allowed not to leave the ground, or a soldier stay in his barracks.

Indeed, it makes a mockery of one important myth of representative government, which is the disinterestedness of our representatives. We all know that there are perks to being a politician; not only the salary, but also juicy positions on company boards or in the media, social status, and an agreeable closeness to the centres of power. No doubt these are attractive to many, but politicians are supposed to evaluate cases on their merits. All well and good, but a referendum stands in the way of this model; here the politician says "Actually, I don't want to decide; *you* decide and I will implement your decision." The politician wants to interrupt the electoral cycle because he fears that if he goes public with what he thinks is the correct choice, he will be booted out come election time. He can claim to be disinterested with respect to the issues of the debate, but on the other hand has spoiled the theoretical model of democracy by growing too fond of the trappings of office to want to risk being defeated.

At its worst, a referendum shouts about the illegitimacy of the political system. Politicians are in effect saying "I believe such-and-such a decision to be right, and best for the country, but equally I am fully aware that under current circumstances the decision will not be accepted as legitimate by the majority of voters. To be legitimate, the voters themselves will have to play an important role in the decision-making. I am not prepared to subject myself to election, for turkeys-not-voting-for-Christmas-type reasons. So we will have a referendum. And when, as I believe it will, the decision goes against my judgement, and when, as I believe they will, the unwanted consequences of that decision appear, then I shall be able to distance myself from the bad decision — a decision which I could have prevented, had I been sufficiently forthright and willing to make proper use of my constitutional privilege as a legislator."

One often hears the praises sung of certain types of consultative exercise, especially in technocratic circles. For instance, citizens' juries are popular. You select a random group of people, who then get presented with the evidence about some particular hard choice, and then they discuss the issues, and quite often they make pretty wise decisions. What's wrong with such systems? Well, only that we pay politicians to do exactly that. Why elect politicians to do something, and then select citizens' juries to do exactly the same thing? Why have politicians at all in that case?

The form of the referendum influences how much it will disrupt the myths of Parliamentary government. Referendums come in four flavours.

- Government sets question, government sets rules, outcome non-binding.
- Government sets question, government sets rules, outcome binding.
- The law requires a referendum as part of an attempt to change the law or adopt a new one, for example if the constitution is to be amended.
- Citizens can provoke referendums by some process, either to protest against something becoming law, or to promote a new law that government will not implement.

The first two cases, and arguably the third, undermine representative government without devolving much power to voters; in other words, the worst of all worlds. In those cases politicians, unable or unwilling to make a decision, frame the debate and frame the question, and line up, sometimes on party lines, sometimes not, on one side of the question or the other. There is a campaign, and the public are forced, in effect, to cast their votes with one set of politicians or the other. The decision is not the politicians', but the range of choices certainly is.

This elides into the second argument against referendums, that by forcing a decision a decision gets made, but consensus isn't reached. A debate brings people together, however involuntarily. Many democratic decision-making forums or institutions are actually designed to promote debate, not to reach some particular decision. By encountering points of view with which one does not agree, and by having to counter arguments against one's own position, one necessarily has to come to some kind of understanding of the other. This sort of democracy, deliberative democracy, is surely superior to one that merely takes a snapshot of opinion and acts on it. Debate with the aim of getting the best solution to a problem is the important thing; sometimes votes will have to be taken, but not always. I have discussed the notion of deliberative democracy at greater length in a book co-written with David Stevens, *inequality.com*.

But a referendum asks not what the best solution should be, but rather whether some particular solution proposed will or will not be adopted (a rare exception being the Swedish vote in 1957 on three alternative pension plans). The result is not consensus, but a victory for one side over the other.

There other arguments against referendums, none as strong as these. One bad argument often made is that ordinary citizens cannot make sufficiently wise decisions. In response, just look at Switzerland, a very direct democracy whose decision-making is as sensible as anywhere you'd care to name. The argument is sometimes modified to say that individual decisions are reasonably well-made, but actually you don't get *coherent* decision-making with referendums. Referendums could trample over treaty obligations, financial common sense, or merely contradict other referendum results as public opinion is notoriously volatile. Well, possibly (though again Switzerland looks like a good counterexample). But anyway, the average European country holds referendums very sparingly; Britain, to reiterate, has held one national one. The chances of one decision made by referendum seriously screwing up the whole of government policymaking, especially when the government makes the rules and sets the question, are small. The argument, which may be good in general, does not have much purchase in the specific case of Britain.

The Arguments in Britain

Well, you pays your money and you takes your choice. The arguments for referendums seem to be at least matched by arguments against, but if we assume that there ought to be at least some positive reason for constitutional innovation, it's not obvious that there was a stronger justification for a referendum in 1975 than to hold the Labour Party together. The arguments leading up to 1975 were almost entirely contingent ones. And if the principle of a referendum was hostage to the political accidents of the time, then it probably follows that the rules governing the actual referendum would be too. We shall consider that question in the next chapter.

Chapter Four
The Rules

Consulting the People

If, in a representative democracy, a referendum gets called for pragmatic reasons, as with Britain's referendum of 1975, then one would expect the rules to be crafted in order to make the right result even more likely. Why leave anything to chance? The people will be consulted: yes, but on terms agreed by those in power. It is the rules that determine the game and, even though the outcome remains uncertain, the balance of probabilities can be adjusted in one direction or the other.

Upon gaining power in February 1974, Labour were committed to consulting the people on the question of renegotiated EEC membership, assuming that the renegotiations went well enough for the government to recommend them. Such an assumption was more than reasonable; few governments expend time and trouble on negotiations without announcing a triumph at the end of them. More to the point, any other course of action in 1975 would require Wilson to make a decision on EEC membership—which is precisely what he was determined not to do.

Traditionally, 'consulting the people' meant a general election with the campaign focused on the topic in question—as when Heath consulted the people about who should run Britain, though the answer he got was not what he wanted. There are, however, two obvious difficulties with this doctrine.

The first is that general election campaigns are hard to keep to a single topic, as Heath discovered. We have seen in our own time campaigns develop unpredictable lives of their own. In 2005, virtually all commentators expected a campaign centred on Tony Blair's leadership, the unpopularity of the war in Iraq and a supposed lack of trust in him; actually, Blair only featured at the end of the campaign. There was some movement of seats from Labour to the anti-war Liberal Democrats, but it was not the campaign the pundits expected.

In 1974-5, Europe featured a long way down the voters' lists of concerns—it is one of those areas of policy that exercises politicians, not their constituents. So there would be a genuine problem in focusing a general election debate on the EEC, as the voters would be sure to want to hear about what *they* believed to be the big issues of the day, inflation, unemployment and the unions.

Second, how could voters make a straightforward choice on the EEC topic, given the way that the issues cut across party lines? The Liberals were in favour of membership. The Tories were overwhelmingly in favour, though the enthusiasm of some of them was muted, and there was a hard core of antis. The Labour leadership was split but officially in favour; the lower echelons of the party were against, with a large pro minority. Only outside England was there a serious anti-EEC choice. If a general election is to decide a great issue, then the serious parties surely need to be lined up on either side.

In the particular context of the mid-70s, there was a third point, and it seems that this loomed largest. There had already been two elections the previous year. The prospect of another filled everyone, voter and politician alike, with horror. The political classes were very wary of turning everyone off. No-one, even those who were opposed to the idea of a referendum, seriously considered that the Government, with its majority of 3, should take the risk of going to the country once more.

So, given that a general election was out, and that consultation was a manifesto pledge, and that ignoring the pledge would split the party, the only option left was an unprecedented referendum. Consequently, in January 1975, while the renegotiations were still underway, Cabinet agreed that when they were concluded, the outcome would be put to the people in a single focused question. The national referendum, conditional on the renegotiation, was born.

The Winning Post

But the fact of holding a referendum only opened up a series of questions about the form it should take. For instance, what should constitute victory? Should a particular margin of victory be required? It might be thought that, particularly on constitutional issues such as the shift in sovereignty away from Parliament that EEC membership had entailed, more than a simple majority of votes would be needed (after all, a simple majority might be a transient matter). Sometimes, as in Switzerland, there needs to be not only a majority of voters in favour, but also a majority of voting areas, constituencies, regions or cantons. In other words, the bar could be set as high as a particular level of majority, or as low as a simple majority.

There are other tricks that one can slip into the rules of a referendum to make passage easier or harder. The majority may have to be of all voters, rather than just those who vote. Or the turnout may need to reach some threshold, say 50% of all voters, before the vote can be counted as valid (this can be a stiff hurdle for a referendum). Indeed, Tory MP Peter Emery unsuccessfully moved an amendment to nullify the referendum by demanding a two thirds turnout, citing the Danish referendum as precedent. And having consulted the people, do the politicians have to abide by the result of the consultation? Could the result be ignored?

In this case there was only one realistic attitude to take. Britain's constitution, being uncodified, is very flexible. No Parliament, at that point, could bind a future one. So just as there was nothing to stop there being a referendum if Parliament willed it, there was equally nothing to stop Parliament from ignoring the result if it chose. The result couldn't, strictly, be binding.

On the other hand, Wilson committed the Government to abide by the result, which again was sensible; after all, why go to the trouble and expense of a referendum if you then ignore it? Raising the possibility in advance that you might ignore the result would be bound to skew turnout, legitimacy and possibly even the balance of the result itself, in unpredictable ways.

Finally, one had to be mindful of Labour's tiny majority. There were a few Tory rebels opposed to membership, and a larger number of Labour rebels in favour. Doubtless very few of these would ignore a whipped vote on a clear-cut referendum result. But if there was a low turnout for the referendum, or a close result, then the Parliamentary arithmetic would be susceptible to alteration by only a few rebels. If the referendum was indecisive, then whatever the rules, the real decision would be made by MPs in the Commons. In particular, the pro-Europe majority in Parliament was sufficiently large to block whatever legislation was required to bring Britain out in the event of a 'no' vote, albeit at the cost of tearing the Labour Party apart.

The Polls

Meanwhile, a remarkable thing had happened. The polls, strongly against membership, often with enormous majorities, since 1967, suddenly flipped. At the beginning of 1975, 50% told Gallup that Britain had been wrong to join the EEC, as opposed to 31% who thought the decision was correct, while 41% would vote to leave, as against 33% who would vote to stay in. This solid opposition had been robust for eight years, and was what prompted constitutional conservatives like Powell and Foot to support the novelty of a referendum.

But in March 1975, when the renegotiated settlement was commended by Wilson and Callaghan, the numbers changed. 37% said they would vote to leave, while 45% would vote to stay in. All pollsters found majorities — large and growing larger — for remaining in the EEC.

No doubt Wilson's recommendation helped with the positive vote. Many voters had no idea of what was being renegotiated, or why, or why it was important for Britain (56% of voters, as late as April 1975, were totally ignorant of the new terms). Indeed, in a rather splendid and wonderfully inexplicable result, those who had switched from anti to pro knew less, on their own admission, than those who had been pro all along. The authority of a Prime Minister should never be underestimated.

Pollsters may also have been asking the wrong questions. People were more willing to say that Britain shouldn't join than they were to say that it had made a mistake when it had joined. Once in, they did not want to say that Britain should take active steps to leave. And putting the complex and hypothetical question *If the Government negotiated new terms for Britain's membership of the Common Market and they thought it was in Britain's interests to remain a member, how would you vote then – to stay in or leave it?* as Gallup did on a number of occasions, led to majorities of well over two to one for staying in as early as August 1974. A question as hypothetical as that one is surely unreliable, but attention to the answers Gallup received should have given the anti-Europe camp some pause for thought.

By May, polling data were very clear cut. To the surprise of many, the pro-Europe camp had established a considerable lead, and the antis were leaking votes all the time. If the polls were reliable, the referendum was going to yield a 'yes' vote by a comfortable margin.

Resources

Ironically, the increasing disparity in the polls between the 'yes' and 'no' camps sorted out what might have been a tricky set of negotiations about the amount of money that could be spent. In America, constitutional provision for free speech has been interpreted in such a way that there are relatively few limits on the amount of money that people and parties standing for office can raise and spend. The result is an extraordinary distortion of democracy, where billionaires can build up giant campaign funds, and lesser mortals with merely huge fortunes have to spend two or three years prior to each election fundraising rather than actually running the country.

Most other countries are sensitive to the problems that such rampant spending can create. In the UK, there are strict limits on the amount of money that can be spent during an election, and although there are certain ways round the regulation (for example, an interview with a party leader on the TV news will be seen by more voters in a given constituency than will read the party leaflets), punishment of actual contravention of the rules is stiff and swift.

With the referendum, new rules were required (if for no other reason than there were no candidates who could be charged with breaching spending limits). The problem in drafting the bill was that the pro camp had much more money than the antis. Most major industrial concerns, as well as two and a half of the three major parties, were wholeheartedly in favour of retaining membership. The only hope for substantial donations to the antis was a few trade unions. The disparity raised questions about whether the campaigns should be subsidised; in this way, constitutional novelty begets constitutional novelty.

By the time the financial rules were being drafted, the 'yes' camp was less concerned with winning the vote, which was almost in the bag, then ensuring that the vote provided enough legitimacy to silence the critics. It was therefore essential that the anti campaign was at least well enough funded to make a fist of it. The antis, on the other hand, were just desperate for money. So it was mutually agreed there would be no upper limit to what could be spent, but that the government should subsidise both camps, by printing and distributing one pamphlet for each camp, and also in cash to the tune of £125,000. This was less levelling the playing field than correcting the slope by a degree or two, but it was a compromise eagerly accepted, for different reasons, by the two sides.

Collective Responsibility

Given that the Government was going to distribute free pamphlets for the two camps, the question naturally arose of whether it would include a third, giving the Government line (and if so, what line that would be). The anti-marketeers were in favour of Governmental silence on the topic, but realistically — as Callaghan had argued right from the beginning of negotiations — having spent so much time and effort negotiating, the Government couldn't be silent. It had to recommend them. Wilson announced in December that he would commend the new terms to the electorate following their agreement.

So constitutional novelty begot even more novelty. Because a substantial proportion of the Cabinet opposed membership, a strong line in favour of membership would cause havoc thanks to the idea of collective responsibility; up to a third of the cabinet could have resigned. Collective responsibility is a venerable British doctrine that states that all members of a Cabinet take equal responsibility for any decision, even ones which they in fact opposed. Arguments go on in Cabinet all the time no doubt, but once a decision has been taken, the losers tacitly agree to support the decision and work for its implementation. If they remain in the Cabinet, they are deemed thereby to support the decision; if they cannot support the decision, they must quit.

A number of pro-marketeers wanted collective responsibility to stay, as it would have had two effects. First, those anti-marketeers who wished to preserve their careers would remain in the Cabinet and therefore be lost to the 'no' campaign. And second, those who *did* choose to jump ship could be portrayed as marginalised figures. Perhaps a more sensible, less partisan reason was that, with a majority of 3, given by a grudging electorate, the Government wasn't strong enough for its senior figures to be attacking each other in public. But given his split party and shaky position, Wilson was going one step at a time; he suspended collective responsibility in January 1975. In this very rare move, Cabinet members were free to voice dissent, and to campaign against their own Government's policy in the forthcoming referendum. This hardly did the Government any good, though whether it could have survived mass resignations that would otherwise have resulted is doubtful.

It was an extraordinary state of affairs, without precedent since the 30s. The Wilson rules only covered general debate; collective responsibility remained for Parliamentary business. Similarly, ministers had to carry on their normal day-to-day affairs in Europe while professing the Government's official position. And, finally, Wilson forbade ministers to make personal attacks on fellow ministers, or to confront fellow ministers directly, on the same platform. Wilson was worried about his fractious lieutenants, and with good reason.

Britain's New Deal in Europe

By the end of May, postie was struggling under the weight of the three pamphlets distributed free of charge. We'll cover the pro and anti documents in the relevant chapters below, but the Government's was called *Britain's New Deal in Europe*[1], and contained a little less argument than the others, and a little more explanation, about the referendum, what the referendum was about, why Britain was having one (well, not the real reason), what the Common Market was, and what the new deal consisted of. For the rest, argument took the general form of reassurances.

The arguments came under three headings, helpfully capitalised in the text like an 18th century novel, oddly conjoined as in a child's essay: FOOD and MONEY and JOBS. With respect to food, secure supplies had been ensured for shoppers at fair prices, and the CAP now supposedly worked more flexibly for the benefit of housewives and farmers in Britain. The rampant inflation of food prices since Britain joined the EEC was explained as the result of steep rises across the world (there was some basis to that claim, thanks to the oil shocks). With respect to money, the pamphlet claimed that Britain's contribution to the EEC budget was manageable where it wasn't before (although it wasn't long before Mrs Thatcher was negotiating another rebate, which Mr Blair is still struggling to preserve). With respect to jobs, they had been made safer because of the putting on hold of economic and monetary union, and Britain was free to pursue its own tax and regional policies (including leaving unpopular VAT off food).

The reassuring noises took up most of the pamphlet. The Commonwealth, far from being against the EEC (as it had been in 1962), was for it, although by then few cared one way or the other (Wilson being an odd internationalist exception). The reduction in Parliamentary sovereignty was explained away: no nation in 1975 could hope to be completely sovereign; Britain had a veto in the Council of Ministers if legislation against the national interest came down from Brussels; Parliament could always repeal the Act that brought us

---

[1] This, and the other two pamphlets, are reproduced in Butler & Kitzinger, *The 1975 Referendum*, pp. 290-304.

into the EEC; Parliament had already accepted the renegotiated terms by a big majority (though this last was a bit of a *non sequitur*).

If Britain voted 'no', it would be an outsider looking in. There would be uncertainty, a reduction in foreign investment, exports to the EEC countries would be handicapped, unemployment and inflation would be worse, and Britain would have no say in the development of the EEC, which, in or out, would inevitably affect its economy. If Britain voted 'yes', on the other hand, it would be larded with European money.

According to a Harris poll just before the referendum itself, about seven in ten voters had seen the document, and one in four had read it from cover to cover. Not too good, then, that only 6% said it had 'helped their understanding of the debate'. Hmm.

Counting

In any large-scale enterprise, it is never easy to predict the sticking points. With the referendum—where one might expect finance to be trickiest—the most problematic area was counting the votes and announcing the results. There was an obvious basis for counting: the mechanisms used in general elections, used twice in the previous year. Each Parliamentary constituency could have counted the votes and announced the results. All the administrative support was in place and rehearsed in procedure.

The pro-Europeans saw two difficulties with the obvious. The first was that the newly resurgent nationalists (in 1970, there had been one nationalist MP; by October 1974, the combined Parliamentary forces of the Scottish National Party and Plaid Cymru was 14), together with some of the Northern Irish parties, were opposed to the EEC, and the polls suggested that any or all of the three countries could vote 'no'. If EEC membership was in effect confirmed by an English 'yes' against a Scottish, Welsh and Northern Irish 'no', that would add another grievance to the nationalists' list. And if the vote were done on the basis of Parliamentary constituency, then it would be possible to work out the votes for the four home nations.

Secondly, many pro-European Labour MPs had quarrelled with their local parties, and they worried that if their constituency vote was 'no', that would be seized upon by their party members as an excuse to deselect them. This sounded far-fetched and paranoid at the time, but within a few years such attempts to deselect right wing MPs were routine.

There was also a third reason put forward. Roy Jenkins wanted a single national count because a few early 'no' declarations in a regionalised poll could cause a run on the pound. There is no record of anyone ever taking this argument seriously.

It proved impossible to discover any sensible way of counting the votes that would prevent anyone from working out how the four nations voted. The only realistic way was a national poll with a single announcement of the gross numbers, but inevitably there would have to be some regionalisation of the counting, and the figures from the regional counts would be bound to leak. However, a compromise was cooked up to save the bacon of Labour MPs; the counting of votes, and the announcement of the results, would be done on a county-by-county basis in England and Wales, on a regional basis in Scotland, and Northern Ireland would have a single count over the whole province. This meant that only three MPs risked the embarrassment of being shown conclusively to be out of touch with their constituents: Stephen Ross (pro-European Liberal, from the Isle of Wight, which was both a county and a constituency), Donald Stewart (anti-European SNP, from the Western Isles, a Scottish region and a constituency), and former Liberal leader Jo Grimond (pro-European: his constituency of Orkney and Shetland comprised two entire Scottish regions).

Despite the administrative chaos this risked, the compromise was accepted, although not until several weeks of wrangling had drifted by. No doubt the fact that the compromise met the threat to MPs' own seats, rather than the wider issue of national unity, helped its acceptance. It seemed to occur to no-one that the information on how people voted should be in the public domain, however inconvenient to a few MPs that would be.

The Date

There seemed no reason to hang around. The Government was fed up of the whole business. The voters, who had been dragged to the polls twice in 1974, and who were pretty fed up with politics, politicians, trade unions, oil sheiks, strikes, Northern Ireland, inflation and unemployment, were even less keen on another spell of keen political debate. Enthusiasts for both the 'yes' and the 'no' causes were wary of boring everyone. Harold Wilson wanted the referendum held as soon as possible. The Referendum Act became law on May 7th, 1975, setting the date to be June 5th. Again, administrative sense was sacrificed to politics; the new Scottish regional authorities, which were to take responsibility for the counts to spare the blushes of pro-European Labour MPs, actually only came into being officially on May 16th.

The Question

The way a question is asked, of course, can skew the outcome—although many psephologists maintain that this is something of a myth if the campaign has been open, full and well-publicised. Nevertheless, the pollsters were keen to investigate: a series of questions posed by National Opinion Polls in February had shown quite some variation (Table 3). The arguments boiled down to two. Some parts of the civil service wanted some explanatory text setting out the Government's position in the question. The second, more trivial but strangely more serious, issue was how to refer to the EEC. The pro-Europeans wanted 'the European Community', which was felt to elicit warm, positive feelings; the antis preferred 'the Common Market', which didn't. In the end, there was compromise on both these questions: a small preamble was decided on, and both referring terms for the EEC were put in, though the subversive nature of the latter was signified by its inclusion being only parenthetic.

So, finally, thirty years after the first serious moves to European union, eighteen years after the signing of the treaty, fourteen years after Britain first applied to join, two and a half years after it actually *had* joined, six months after a referendum became official Government policy, and three months after the announcement of the renegotiated terms, the British people were to be consulted on the EEC for the first time, with the following question.

> The Government have announced the results of the renegotiation of the United Kingdom's terms of membership of the European Community.
>
> DO YOU THINK THAT THE UNITED KINGDOM SHOULD STAY IN THE EUROPEAN COMMUNITY (THE COMMON MARKET)?

Table 3: Different Questions, Different Responses[2]

Question	Choice	'Yes' or 'In' majority (%)
Do you accept the Government's recommendation that the United Kingdom should come out of the Common Market?[3]	Yes/No	0.2
Should the United Kingdom come out of the Common Market?	Yes/No	4.6
	In/Out	10.8
Should the United Kingdom stay in the Common Market?	Yes/No	13.2
Do you accept the Government's recommendations that the United Kingdom should stay in the Common Market?	Yes/No	18.2
The Government recommends the acceptance of the renegotiated terms of British membership of the Common Market. Should the United Kingdom stay in the Common Market?	Yes/No	11.2
Her Majesty's Government believes that the nation's best interests would be served by accepting the favourably renegotiated terms of our continued membership of the Common Market. Should the United Kingdom stay in the Common Market?	Yes/No	16.2

---

[2] Source: NOP poll, Feb 1975, quoted by Butler & Kitzinger p. 60.
[3] Note that when this poll was taken, the result of the renegotiation was still in doubt (in theory if not in fact).

Chapter Five

The Yes Camp

The Arguments

The arguments deployed by the yes camp, as set out in their officially-distributed pamphlet *Why You Should Vote Yes* (anonymous, but largely rewritten from early drafts by Roy Jenkins), were surprisingly low key. The first was particularly underwhelming: given that Britain had wrestled for so long to get into the community, surely it should avoid the agony of pulling out. Furthermore, membership *per se* wouldn't solve Britain's manifold problems, but instead would provide the best framework for success. Whether one should sacrifice sovereignty and a thousand years of history for a mere framework was left unanswered.

The positive arguments were a bit Miss Worldy. 'Our friends want us to stay in'. The Prime Ministers of Australia, New Zealand and Canada were quoted – perhaps a tacit acceptance that the only countries that would not rub voters up the wrong way were the former white colonies; no quotes from Germans, Indians, Americans or Jamaicans. And whereas our friends wanted us in, 'outside we would be alone in a harsh, cold world, with none of our friends offering to revive old partnerships'. This seems to imply that 'our friends' were hardly such at all, fair-weather friends at best. Could Jenkins have complained had voters drawn the conclusion that Britain should tell its 'friends' to sod off and join the Soviet Union instead?

'Staying in protects our jobs' was a paean to large markets and juicy regional policies. 'Secure food at fair prices'; this argument, in the context of the CAP, was tendentious at best.

The pamphlet also countered the no camp's main arguments. 'Why can't we go it alone?' The sovereignty argument, it was maintained, was false, 'dry legal theory'. The 'real test' is power in the world, and the argument was made, plausibly, that Britain's power would be enhanced by being in the Community. This hardly proved the sovereignty argument false; rather it side-stepped the problem, arguing that sovereignty was a red herring and that power mattered more (not a *prima facie* silly thing to say). But it had the merit of *nearly* taking on the no camp at its strongest point. The other counterargument, 'Our traditions are safe', was an irrelevant attempt to scotch the permanent silly-season rumours that the Queen would be deposed. Perhaps the most telling passage in the pamphlet, in the conclusion, rubbished the no camp with an *ad hominem* attack—which laid the foundation for much of the campaign (see Chapter Seven).

According to the aforementioned Harris poll, 82% of people saw the 'yes' pamphlet (more than saw the other two), 30% read it cover to cover (ditto), and 10% said it helped their understanding (ditto, though still a pitifully small proportion).

The Organisation

The referendum posed an intriguing problem for both camps, in that mass campaigning had always been the preserve, indeed the skill and *raison d'être*, of the major political parties, but the parties stood aloof from the contest. New institutions were required, new coalitions needed to appear, and be nimble enough to reconfigure themselves as circumstances changed. In the end, each camp produced a single umbrella organisation to coordinate many smaller ones; a lucky break, as it was not at all clear what would happen if either camp had split. Would it affect the legitimacy of a referendum result to have two yes camps or two no camps arguing amongst themselves rather than the opposition? In 1975, we never found out.

The yes camp was better placed, having been in the position for decades of having to campaign to change things; the no camp, in contrast, had supported what was the status quo until 1972–3, and so had had less reason to mobilise. The European Movement had been devoted to campaigning for a European union including Britain since 1948, and helpfully had half a million pounds in the bank. But its hardball tactics had made its name mud with Labour Party activists. A new organisation would be required.

Britain in Europe (BIE) was the vehicle that arrived, which managed, not without difficulty, to take over many of the resources of the European Movement while sidelining its controversial officials. Altogether it raised (largely from donations from business) and spent somewhere in the region of £1.5m, a tiny quantity from today's perspective although at the time more than any party had spent on a general election. Most of the money went on advertising, PR and printing. BIE's pitch was to present a united front of politicians from all three parties, showing a sensible, moderate majority overwhelmingly in favour. Rallies were held all around Britain in the run-up to the vote. Less traditionally, some American campaigning techniques were toyed with, but many were embarrassed by slick TV broadcasts and mass telephoning. There was even a rather effective logo, at the cost, thought outrageous by many insiders, of £1,700, of a dove in flight in Union Jack colours—cleverly preventing the no campaign monopolising the flag.

The campaign bred camaraderie among the party politicians. Feelings ran high within the Labour party, and the small pro-European group felt increasingly embattled. Consequently, the Tories and Liberals in BIE, comfortable in their respective parties, were keen to make life as easy for the Labour members as possible.

It was more or less agreed that the campaign should be as party-independent as was feasible, although it was also gradually realised by the yes camp that the Tory organisation was one of their greatest assets. The Tories, even post-Heath, saw entry to Europe as their achievement (Thatcher had served in the Cabinet at the time of entry); that enthusiasm, combined with the legendary Tory ability to drum up enthusiastic volunteers was a trump card. The biggest obstacle to mobilising the blue-rinse brigade was a view that the whole mess was Harold Wilson's problem, and why should they sort it out for him?

The Liberals were almost entirely pro-Europe, and liaised with BIE closely. There were some complaints that their campaign was more party political than those of the others. Labour's pro-Europeans were under pressure, but that seemed to create an *esprit de corps* that made them an effective unit. Cabinet members Jenkins and Shirley Williams took the lead, while lieutenants such as William Rodgers and Dickson Mabon organised committees actively.

The Confederation of British Industry, the employers' organisation, was pro and helpful. The few pro-European trade unions (including the shopworkers' USDAW, and the railwaymen's NUR), with their love of unpronounceable acronyms, organised under the banner of the Trade Union Alliance for Europe (TUAE). BIE had strong links with the EEC itself, through commissioners Sir Christopher Soames and George Thomson, and used information fed to it from Brussels, but it tried to avoid involving any actual foreigners, almost as if it was worried in case they breathed garlic over the electors. The press was almost all pro-European (yes, this really is Britain, though it is a little like writing about a parallel universe), but their enthusiasm for an issue that was complex and, frankly, boring was limited. In contrast, a pious note was injected by a young enthusiast, currently unemployed having lost his Parliamentary seat in 1974, called John Selwyn Gummer, who mobilised almost all the Anglican bishops, and organised prayers for Europe in almost half the churches in the country (bless!).

At the local level, there was an enthusiastic, if ramshackle, dads' army of volunteers in semi-autonomous organisations given a steer from above. Outside England, with a 'no' vote expected, nationalist sentiment was strong. Even Northern Ireland's Unionists had pulled away from the Tories to establish a separate anti-EEC identity, their Toryism trumped by their visceral affection for Westminster; many suspected Europe to be a Papist plot. On the nationalist side, Sinn Fein was anti-EEC, as it recognised current borders, while the Social Democratic and Labour Party was pro, because it considered the EEC might be able to create a supra-national entity in which the Irish border would be rendered irrelevant. Because of the troubles, Northern Ireland had had its bellyful of referendums and votes to decide all sorts of things, and the anticipation of a low turnout stifled interest. Northern Ireland in Europe spent a mere £8,500.

The Scotland in Europe campaign was set up in parallel with BIE, and held at arm's length, on the assumption that the Scottish campaign should be untainted by Sassenach treachery. Its own pamphlet played down the capitalist overtones of the EEC. Wales in Europe was also autonomous, and its bilingual campaign literature emphasised the possibility of using the EEC to help devolve powers downwards, an argument that appealed to a large minority in the nominally-anti Plaid Cymru.

In England, BIE took over many of the European Movement's local groups. Other groups were formed from scratch by volunteers who often rather surprised themselves with their enthusiasm, and indeed with what could be achieved on a shoestring. In other places, Tory and Liberal Parties formed the backbone of the local group; some of these were caught distributing party literature alongside the BIE material. Most spent a few hundred pounds up to the low thousands locally, perhaps adding up to a quarter of a million in total on top of the national spend of BIE. The local groups were advised to ape the name of the national organisation, thereby mobilising local pride: Pudsey in Europe, Basingstoke in Europe, the Forest of Dean in Europe, etc. On no account, they were told, must they call themselves Little Bumstead *for* Europe, because that was an own goal; they would find themselves opposed by the patriotic-sounding Little Bumstead for *Britain*. The independent-minded burghers of Fareham in Hampshire immediately ignored this sage advice, and Fareham for Europe was born. Perhaps they thought it was obvious that Fareham was already in Europe, and that the point was more to do with enthusiasm for being there? We shall never know.

The Personalities

It was the politicians who were most prominent in the campaign—a handy change from a likely modern referendum campaign, where identical grey politicos would rub shoulders with people from *EastEnders* and her on the left out of Atomic Kitten and feel grateful for the exposure. The yes camp was blessed, if that was the word, with many high profile politicians, including all three party leaders. Some of the major campaigners were the following.

Edward Heath

We have met Ted already, of course, the man who can take the most responsibility for Britain's entry into the EEC, as significant a contribution to British history as any politician of his generation. A difficult man, at the time of the referendum on the backbenches, we haven't so far mentioned his amazing qualities as a renaissance man, being a talented musician and world-class yachtsman. Another difference from today's politics: a politician with outside interests. It is hard to imagine David Cameron winning the Sydney to Hobart race, for example, as Heath had done as Leader of the Opposition in 1969. On the other hand, it is equally hard to imagine any of today's political anoraks, blinkered as they are, being as bitter after political failure as Heath. For example, William Hague, after his extremely unsuccessful career as Tory leader came to an end at the age of forty, cheered up considerably, wrote a biography of Pitt the Younger, and learned the piano as a publicity stunt. Heath, by contrast, pulled his face into a sort of bored sneer, whereupon the wind changed and the expression stayed with him until his death in 2005.

Roy Jenkins

Jenkins, the son of a Welsh miner, was the unofficial leader of the pro-European movement. At the time of the referendum he was Home Secretary, a post which he had also used in the 60s to promote a famous liberal regime; he had also been Chancellor. He was grand, impossibly grand, a *bon viveur* fond of ladies and claret, author of scholarly political biographies, some of which, as he was fond of reminding people, were the standard texts. He had always nurtured ambitions of the leadership, although it surely is doubtful he ever could have made it. He always put his failure down to his natural diffidence and lack of ruthlessness, which shows that, if he knew all there was to know about Asquith or Gladstone, he knew relatively little about himself.

Harold Wilson

The Prime Minister, and supreme political operator of his day, he had won four of the last five general elections. No visionary, his formidable skills and intelligence, carefully concealed under his Gannex raincoat, were primarily devoted to holding the Labour Party, hopelessly split between left and right, together. That he could do this at all was an achievement, as he had been explicitly the creature of the left when he succeeded Hugh Gaitskell. Unfortunately he was paranoid about plots, although people were always plotting against him so his paranoia came in handy more than once. He had explicitly ruled out the use of a referendum in the general election campaign of 1970, pointing out that he never changed his mind because the polls go up and down. Yeah, right.

As Prime Minister, Wilson tried to stay above the fray. Having organised the renegotiation, he had perforce to recommend the results to the British people, but he kept clear of BIE. This was partly to preserve the impression of statesmanship, but also partly tactical; the theory was that the zealots of the pro and anti camps would convert no-one, but Wilson could pose as the sensible moderate man who might swing waverers from no to yes. However, this idea backfired as he had no independent platform on which to speak; the Labour Party certainly would not lend its imprimatur to what would be a series of pro-European broadcasts or speeches. As a result, his influence on the campaign was rather less than he might have liked. While the result was in doubt he was keen on distance, but as the ground shifted positively in the direction of the yes camp, he missed the opportunity to appear prominently on the winning side.

Jeremy Thorpe

The young, dapper, popular leader of the Liberal Party had also opposed the use of referendums in 1970, but in 1975 was not averse to using this one to promote his waxing party. Britain was fed up with Wilson and Heath, and Thorpe provided a raffish contrast. Unfortunately, as a gay man in a homophobic world, his days were numbered, and a bizarre court case, in which Thorpe was accused, and acquitted, of plotting to murder a former lover, ended his career. The lover, a man named Norman Scott, became briefly famous, as did his dog Rinka (which had actually been killed), although the abiding memory of the whole episode was Peter Cook's spoof of Mr Justice Cantley's incredibly biased (in favour of Thorpe) summing-up in the case. Worth remembering, when we get nostalgic for the good old days, that a gay affair could end a political career in disgrace as recently as 1976.

Margaret Thatcher

The lady who needs no introduction. Actually, in 1975 she was still little-known, and Britain's small-c conservative voters were still coming to terms with a woman party leader, never mind a potential Prime Minister. Her involvement in the campaign was minimal, partly because she was a party leader, partly because there was obvious good sense in letting Heath do most of the work. She was not yet the overwhelming force that she was to become, and it is curious how little she features in the referendum (she received quite a bit of criticism from the press towards the end of the campaign for her invisibility, believe it or not). The personal chemistry between her and Heath tended to dominate, so when she shared a platform with Heath in April, the press ignored the campaign and instead wrote it up as the reconciliation of Ted and Maggie. At the risk of stating the obvious, that was not true.

Shirley Williams

At the time of the referendum Williams was Secretary of State for Prices and Consumer Affairs — these being the days when government control of the microeconomy was at a level nowadays unthinkable. A sort of political Miss Marple (at least in the Margaret Rutherford incarnation), Williams cultivated an oh-I-left-my-hat-on-the-train scattiness, but she was one of the more intelligent people in a notably brainy Cabinet. There was heavy politicking within the BIE campaign, and Williams was a victim; there were dark mutterings that she was pushed out of the media limelight by friends of Jenkins.

Jim Callaghan

An avuncular, slow-speaking politician from a trade union background, Callaghan looked like Mr Magoo and had been a major player in the Labour Party for some time, often suspected by Wilson of plotting against him. He was the only politician in modern times to hold all four major offices of state, including being Prime Minister from 1976–79; at the time of the referendum he was in the key position of Foreign Secretary.

This meant that he conducted the renegotiations. Callaghan was a difficult man if he felt under pressure or out of his comfort zone (Benn's diaries report him shouting "you clot!" at a heckler in a Labour Party debate on the EEC), though brilliant once he was at home in the milieu. Characteristically, he had begun the EEC renegotiations very badly in 1974, offending virtually everybody, but had found his feet and eventually worked well with his European counterparts, and seems never seriously to have considered the possibility of not reaching a conclusion and recommending it to the voters.

His position in the campaign, as the man who had actually conducted the renegotiation, was similar to Wilson's. As often in his career, he portrayed himself as the sensible man in the middle, and memorably argued that in the referendum there were three positions, the pro-marketeers, the anti-marketeers and the truth. One assumes that Callaghan represented the truth in this scheme. However, having avoided BIE, like Wilson he struggled to find an outlet for his influence.

Vic Feather

In the days when trade union leaders played the same role in politics as Great Aunts do in the works of P.G. Wodehouse, Lord Feather was President of the Trade Union Alliance for Europe. He had retired as General Secretary of the Trade Union Congress in 1973, but still had major face recognition. The *Private Eye* cover of 11th August, 1972, showed a dialogue between Heath and Feather: Heath begins "Who d'you think's running this country?" to which Feather replies "ME!" and a smiling Heath concludes "Thank God! For one awful moment I thought I was!" The unions being split, the retired Feather (indeed he died the next year), actually got more coverage than his former colleagues — particularly when he accused Tony Benn of being a flat-Earther. Feather was a great boon to the yes campaign, as his agreeable down-to-(round)-Earth manner meant that he filled a gap. Compared with the insufferably grand Jenkins, or the stiff Heath, Feather's common touch prevented the yes campaign from alienating ordinary voters.

The Others

- **George Brown**. By now, the weird and wonderful Brown was Lord George-Brown, possibly so-titled in case he ever drunkenly forgot who he was. Having lost his seat in 1970, he was drifting further from the Labour Party (he quit entirely in 1976) and used at least some of the campaign to argue for a coalition government to deal with Britain's horrendous economic problems. Although his contribution to Britain's joining the EEC had not been small, he wasn't prominent in the referendum campaign, except for a television programme in which he and anti-marketeer Clive Jenkins were driven round Europe in a bus, arguing all the way. But as that programme was seen by nearly nine million people, most of whom found it jolly entertaining, he may have swung more votes than other more visible campaigners.

- **Tom Jackson**. General Secretary of the Union of Post Office Workers, chiefly famous for a splendid moustache, though also blessed with a sense of humour.

- **Reg Prentice**. Secretary of State for Education and Science, an outspoken right winger whose patience with the Labour Party was fast running out (he joined the Tories in 1977 and indeed served in the first Thatcher government). He had initially opposed the EEC on the grounds of its being a grouping of rich nations, but was converted to the European cause upon discovering that its attitude towards the developing world (specifically the former French colonies) was relatively enlightened and that it stumped up a decent amount of overseas aid.

- **Sir Christopher Soames**. As a son-in-law of Churchill he obviously commanded great respect; as one of Britain's two European Commissioners he was very useful indeed to the BIE campaign.

- **David Steel**. The neat and diminutive Liberal Chief Whip, who was also instrumental in setting up BIE.

- **Willie Whitelaw.** Led the Tory campaign, very prominent in the media (and so was actually more recognised than Roy Jenkins, much no doubt to the latter's chagrin). This campaign was the beginning of his working relationship with Mrs Thatcher — which could have been very sour after she defeated him in the leadership election.

Opinion

The value of these figures for the yes campaign depended on public perceptions of them. Table 4 shows the results of a Harris poll undertaken in early April 1975 (results given in full in Butler & Kitzinger, p. 256), together with an attempt at giving a more subjective view of the politicians in question. The last four columns, then, are my own, though not my own opinions (they are certainly not *assertions*). They are intended to be subjective distillations of the general commentary about them at the time, in the press, by comedians and satirists, other politicians and so on; I haven't generated entries here for those below Shirley Williams, as they were too little known to generate a public image as such. In the *Interesting?* slot, 5 = very interesting, 1 = very boring. In the *Mad?* slot, 1 = weirdly normal, 2 = average, 3 = odd, 4 = barking and 5 = completely Radio Rental.

Notice that the approval ratings are all positive, that at least some of the politicians are interesting, and that the average score in the *Mad?* column is only just above 2. How did that compare with the no camp?

Table 4: Public Attitudes to Leading Figures in the Yes Camp*

Politician	Person known	Respect and like	Don't like	Approval rating**	Good points	Bad points	Interesting?	Mad?
Harold Wilson	97%	42%	23%	+19	Effective	Shifty	2	2
Edward Heath	94	42	21	+21	Musical	Boorish	2	1
Jeremy Thorpe	91	40	11	+29	Charming	Dandified	4	2
Roy Jenkins	82	34	9	+25	Witty	Pompous	4	2
Reggie Maudling	79	26	14	+12	Clever	Sly	3	2
Vic Feather	79	33	15	+18	Common touch without being patronising	Over-mighty	1	2
Jim Callaghan	79	31	11	+20	Avuncular	Dull	2	2
Lord George-Brown	79	28	16	+12	Brilliant	Piss artist	5	4
Shirley Williams	78	33	8	+25	Intelligent	Scatty	4	3
Sir Christopher Soames	57	17	5	+12				
Tom Jackson	56	14	13	+1				
Geoffrey Rippon	55	15	6	+9				
Reg Prentice	53	12	7	+5				

* Taken from Butler & Kitzinger, p. 256. Willie Whitelaw is not included here, as his figures are plainly incorrect in Butler & Kitzinger's version of the table. ** I.e. percentage of people respecting and liking minus the percentage not liking. The rest of the 100% is made up of the percentage of people with no strong opinion and the percentage of people who didn't recognise the figure in question.

Chapter Six
The No Camp

The Arguments

There was a great deal of wrangling over the no camp's official pamphlet, *Why You Should Vote No*; in the end it seems to have been a joint piece of work by Neil Marten, Douglas Jay, Enoch Powell and *Daily Express* journalist George Gale. Of necessity it had to keep clear of one of the chief arguments (for many of its proponents) against the EEC, which was that it was designed to make socialism impossible, and prevent capitalism itself from being challenged. Though many of the more influential members of the no camp subscribed to that argument, particularly Foot, Benn and the trade unionists, the small but vocal Tory element would hardly have wished for it to go out under their names. Indeed, as Anthony King pointed out in his commentary on the referendum, there were two campaigns going on simultaneously — one addressed to the country at large, and another quite separate and covert one to persuade Labour Party activists.

The balance to be achieved in the pamphlet was between worries about the big constitutional issues of sovereignty, independence and democracy, and the smaller issues affecting individual households, such as expected increases in food prices or unemployment. And to be countered was the growing feeling that, now Britain was in, the practical difficulties of pulling out would be too great; this threatened the votes of many people basically sympathetic to the no cause.

Much was made of the sovereignty question of course, the 'right to rule ourselves'. The current arrangements of the EEC were asserted to be the thin end of the wedge; 'it sets out by stages to merge Britain with France, Germany, Italy and other countries into a single nation'. Not only that, but there would be a European Parliament by 1978. And the Common Market couldn't provide for Britain's defence; for this it would still need NATO. This was certainly the simplest of the no arguments to make — we don't want to be pushed around by

Johnny Foreigner—although polling showed it wasn't one that resonated.

The prices argument was the most important. 'All of us, young and old alike, will have to pay', with the splendid *non sequitur* of the subordinate clause implying equal rancour within the EEC for people of all ages. The price of butter would have to be doubled by 1978; the Common Market had deliberately raised a beef mountain of 300,000 tons; food prices in Britain and Ireland had risen by 40% since 1971, but in non-members Norway and Sweden by only 20%. Not only that, but Britons would also have to pay higher taxes to pay for European agriculture. Jobs were also threatened; the drift of industry Southwards would continue, increasingly to the continent, with the government powerless to intervene. It would be particularly bad in Scotland, Wales, Northern Ireland, and the North and West of England, which doesn't leave much.

To counter the pro-European arguments, the no camp's line was to show, using the Government's own figures, that predictions of the benefits of membership were false. The waters here were very muddy, in that poor Government policies stretching back years, the massive hike in oil prices following the 1973 war in the Middle East, and the inability to deal with the problem of strikes were also clearly relevant to Britain's economic performance. The yes camp were on weak ground here, and they knew it. They had always tried to emphasise that membership was a framework for progress, not a panacea, but this sort of nuance gets lost in mass political debate.

Pulling out would be difficult, and there was always the question of life outside. The no camp had to meet this issue: would Britain be a free trading nation, or a protectionist fortress, or what? There was, in truth, little agreement behind the scenes; Benn, for example, sounded increasingly protectionist, while Powell and Peter Shore wanted to restore Britain's traditional status as a trading nation. The pamphlet pointed out that Norway had said no to the EEC in a referendum without the roof falling in, although the obvious flaw was that the Norwegians had never been in the EEC, and so had never had to pull out. Stressing that Britain had a right to pull out, as determined in the debates on the European Communities Act, was true, yet irrelevant to the question of how difficult it would be (I have a legal right to eat my car, but ...).

Taken all in all, the pamphlet was heavier on argument than that of the yes camp, eschewing the folksy touches—perhaps betraying the influence of Enoch Powell, who had helped determine its structure. Part of the problem was that membership had altered the balance between the camps. When Britain was not in the EEC, the pro-Europeans looked like nerdy obsessives who wanted everything to change; now the no camp were playing that role, so to combat that perception it was essential to produce a sensible-sounding and statesmanlike document. To an extent it succeeded, at least in tone, but few were satisfied with the end result. 73% of voters got to see the pamphlet, and 28% read it through, but only 8% said that it helped with their understanding.

The Organisation

At Christmas 1974, Tony Benn morosely surveyed the list of anti-EEC organisations which needed to be welded into a coherent force: the Get Britain Out campaign, the National Referendum Campaign, the Common Market Safeguards Campaign, British Businessmen for World Markets, the Anti-Common Market League and the National Council of Anti-Common Market Organisations[1]. "I must say," he sighed, "it is going to be an awful rag-bag."

Benn's preference was to convert the Labour Party to an anti-EEC stance and work through it. This, of course, was impractical. The whole point of the referendum was to hold the party together; Benn would not have cried into his pipe had the Labour Party lost Jenkins and Williams, but nonetheless the wound to the party would have been serious, as Wilson (not an unadulterated fan of Jenkins himself) understood.

It was the National Referendum Campaign (NRC) that was the analogue of BIE, the coordinator of the various groups. Its problem was the pro-Europeans' domination of the centrist, moderate establishment. Relatively few mainstream politicians were opposed to membership — Benn, Michael Foot, Barbara Castle in the Cabinet, for example — but for various reasons opposition to the EEC thrived at the extremes. So the far right and the far left, both more active in the more polarised politics of thirty years ago, had to be incorporated and coordinated somehow, or, if their views were totally unacceptable, they had to be marginalised and their enthusiasm and manpower sacrificed. The National Council of Anti-Common Market Associations, for instance, was understood to be very right wing,

---

[1] So many and varied were these organisations that Mr Benn, understandably, got slightly confused. It is British *Business* for World Markets, based in Yorkshire, and the National Council of Anti-Common Market *Associations*.

and included officially under the NRC's wing only after much discussion. Many other small and extreme groups were excluded. The Communists and the National Front were rejected, as for less obvious reasons were the Women Against the Common Market, this last being a harmless group headed by former Labour MP Anne Kerr until her untimely death at 48 in 1973.

The two main parts of the NRC were the Common Market Safeguards Campaign (CMSC) established by former Labour Cabinet minister Douglas Jay, and Get Britain Out (GBO), which was what an earlier organisation Keep Britain Out had morphed into, logically enough, after Britain joined. The CMSC was sort of political, and sort of leftish; GBO was sort of business/law and sort of rightish (it was GBO that provided Enoch Powell with his platform to denounce the Tory leadership in the runup to the election in February 1974). They got on like cat and dog; a row had erupted after the CMSC reneged on an alleged promise to fund a bookstore at the 1973 Tory conference, and memberships were torn up. GBO then gained revenge by poaching the CMSC's full-time director Ron Leighton, later to become Labour MP for pro-European Reg Prentice's former constituency.

The Labour Party, below ministerial level, was quite anti, and a shambolic special conference just prior to the referendum came out in favour of a 'no' vote (see Chapter Seven). The Labour Committee for Safeguards on the Common Market was a home for many of Labour's no campaigners. There were strong connections with the CMSC — in fact, the latter was a cross-party offshoot of the former, and the committee kept going after the referendum appeared to settle the matter. Now called the Labour Euro-Safeguards Campaign, under the chairmanship of Austin Mitchell, it is currently savouring the 'no' votes in the French and Dutch referendums of 2005.

The other mainstream parties had small pockets of heterodox opinion. CATOR, the Conservatives Against the Treaty of Rome held the Tory anti-marketeers, although this was less influential given the much larger majority for membership in that party. For completeness, we should mention the Liberal "No" to the Common Market Campaign, but this tiny percentage of a small party was not significant.

The nationalists were the largest parties to declare against membership, so in the regions the NRC could count on the local connections, and street cred, of the Scottish National Party, Plaid Cymru, the United Ulster Unionists and Sinn Fein. However in the upshot, this amounted to rather less than was gleefully anticipated. The SNP, who through the early 70s had built their position up to 30% of the vote in Scotland, enjoyed the anti-Labour and anti-Westminster whammy of opposing membership, but on the other hand Scotland expected to do rather well from the EEC and hence its opposition was not wholehearted. In the end, the leadership made its opportunism explicit: an English 'yes' and a Scottish 'no' would show how the two nations had drifted apart. Plaid Cymru, in contrast, worked well with the Labour left and GBO, although again its ambitions were tempered by hopes for a generous European regional policy. 'No' votes were anticipated in all three nations, although not big enough to offset the expected 'yes' from England.

The trade unions were largely against membership, as mandated by a TUC vote in September 1974, but although some individual leaders were very prominent in the campaign, the unions kept their wallets in their pockets and their members on the leash. After two expensive general election campaigns in the previous year, the wells of their political funds were pretty dry. Overall, they were not a great deal of help.

And it was money that the NRC needed above all. It had a government grant of £125,000, but under its own steam it raised less than £9,000. GBO chipped in £28,000, but not much came from any other source. Taken all in all the no camp had about a tenth of the resources of the yes camp.

Locally, there were rather too many little platoons to go around, and they seem to have spent as much time fighting each other as BIE. There were many charges of communist infiltration, although it is hard to determine whether they were in fact true, or stemmed from paranoia. One small consolation for the democrats in the no camp is that, however successful communist efforts to infiltrate the NRC were, they didn't seem to bring down the government or overthrow capitalism. They never really do. David Butler and Uwe Kitzinger, who conducted extensive qualitative research on the individual experiences of no and yes campaigners, detected much more disillusion among the no campaigners than one would expect simply from the fact that the referendum didn't go their way. The disparity in funds and fundraising with the yes camp carried over to the micro-level; a local group was doing OK if it raised £100.

Urdu and Welsh—to trump the very English Heath where possible. He would argue that only someone who knew Europe as he, Powell, did could understand how the EEC, with its tendency to erode precious national characteristics, was a bad thing for Europe; Powell, the passionate Francophile, would occasionally mischievously claim to be the real pro-European. In 1971, he toured Europe giving lectures, in French, Italian and German, in Lyon, Frankfurt, Turin and the Hague.

Michael Foot

Like Benn and Powell, Michael Foot was a politician in whom independence, combined with intelligence, combined with culture led ultimately to failure. Also from a dissenting dynasty, Foot began as a crusading journalist who came to the attention of Lord Beaverbrook, who made him editor of the *Evening Standard* at the age of 28 (it is safe to say that the paper was a different beast to the one we have now), and first joined parliament in the 1945 landslide. In Labour's great internecine wars of the 1950s, Foot resisted the Labour establishment, preferring oppositional stances. He supported Bevan, though the two eventually fell out, and turned down offers of government jobs under Wilson until 1974, when he became Secretary of State for Employment.

His command of rhetoric was legendary, as was his feel for the history of Britain's labour and dissenting movement. One of his finest hours came in the late 1960s, when in tandem with Powell, he managed to kill a Labour Government bill to reform the House of Lords. The two attacked it for different reasons; Foot was opposed to the undemocratic nature of the proposal to pack the Lords with appointed life peers, while Powell made a conservative case against changing the constitution.

Foot, however, had one quality that Benn and Powell lacked—which is probably the reason he went further than the other two. He had the ability to compromise, and picked fights somewhat more intelligently (Benn called him "fake left" in his diary; Foot referred indignantly to "Bennfoolery" in a letter to the *Guardian*). For that reason, he was a more convincing bridge between left and right of the Labour Party, although unlike Wilson he failed either to keep the party together, or to channel the energies of the left into an electorally productive direction.

Barbara Castle

Left wing Secretary of State for Social Services at the time of the referendum, notorious in British politics for bringing in parking meters and breathalysers, and a confidant of Wilson, she was the most prominent member of the campaign to argue at the microeconomic level that food prices would be adversely affected and foster poverty. Her appeal to the left, however, had been badly damaged by her attempt in 1969 to bring in legislation to regulate the unions. Ironically, having been given short shrift by her enemy Jim Callaghan when he became Prime Minister in 1976, she quit Parliament, bequeathing her seat to Jack Straw, and led the British Labour group in the European Parliament in 1979-85. She was one of the hardest workers in the no camp, making many speeches and broadcasts.

Ian Paisley

The Reverend Doctor Ian Paisley probably takes the controversialist biscuit among the no camp. His ordination has been called into question; his doctorate was honorary, not earned through research, and was awarded by Bob Jones University, a segregationist Christian college which at the time of the award banned black students from its campus (Harvard it ain't). But whether or not he is a real reverend, whether or not he is a real doctor, he is the one and only Ian Paisley (er, well, Ian Paisley Jr is currently an Assembly member for the Democratic Unionist Party).

By 1975, Paisley, then an MP for the United Ulster Unionists, was notorious for bigoted verbal attacks on Catholics, and for being the mouthpiece for the most intransigent and intolerant factions of the Protestant community. Like Benn he was loved by his own people, hated by everyone else. His hoarse roar was a well-known feature of the dreadful polarised politics of Northern Ireland.

Peter Shore

Formerly close to Wilson (he was his PPS in 1965-6), Peter Shore was another earnest intellectual figure, with a quiet voice and nondescript face, saved only from complete immemorability by a loose flop of hair with a life of its own which would turn him momentarily into a political Veronica Lake. He had moved into Benn's circle when he joined MinTech (as the Ministry of Technology was hi-techly called) in 1966, and was a long-time opponent of the EEC. At the time of the referendum, he was Secretary of State for Trade.

Neil Marten

The lack of major politicians to man the barricades catapulted one or two relative unknowns to national fame, at least for the 15 minutes of the campaign. Neil Marten, the Tory MP for Banbury, had been a junior minister under Macmillan and Home, but had also been a long-standing opponent of membership, on the grounds of sovereignty; he had refused office under Heath for that reason. He was a great asset for the no camp, moderate and average, reasonable and unthreatening. He took the post of Chairman of the NRC, and was seen to have done a very good job.

Christopher Frere-Smith

Frere-Smith had leapt to mini-fame as the chair of Keep Britain Out in 1966. He was a solicitor who was not, let us say, publicity-shy; he had been central to the Great Bookstall Controversy between GBO and the CMSC, and had quit the latter organisation in disgust. He had run GBO as an anti- establishment group; one of his populist criticisms was that the whole EEC thing had been stitched up by the establishment, all three major parties ganging up together, giving the British voter no anti-market alternative. However, given the Westminster bias of the no camp, such a position could not be transferred to the referendum campaign (as, for example, the no votes in France and Holland in 2005 were partly driven by a rejection of the pieties and dogmas of political elites). Perhaps as a result, Frere-Smith's attendance record at the NRC's steering committee was patchy, and there were many complaints that GBO was too independent, and not playing a team game.

The Others

- **Douglas Jay.** Chairman of the CMSC, and behind-the-scenes organiser for the no campaign. Former President of the Board of Trade from 1964-7, he was well-connected within the Labour party: his son (TV presenter of *Weekend World*) married Jim Callaghan's daughter (who later became the leader of the House of Lords). He looms large in Conservative mythology as the man who originally coined the phrase "the gentleman in Whitehall really does know better".

- **Clive Jenkins.** Smiling, intelligent and witty General Secretary of the white-collar union the Association of Scientific, Technical and Managerial Staffs (ASTMS), whose sing-song Welsh accent was oft-parodied.
- **Jack Jones.** General Secretary of the Transport and General Workers' Union. With Hugh Scanlon, he practically ran the country, or, rather, prevented it from being run, in the 70s; they were known as the 'terrible twins'.
- **Hugh Scanlon.** President of the Amalgamated Union of Engineering Workers, unlike the austere Jones (whom Scanlon claimed thought he was Jesus), Scanlon was something of a *bon viveur* and 60s celeb. At the famous Chequers tea to discuss Labour's proposed trade union laws in 1969, it was Scanlon to whom Wilson directed his famous remark "Hughie, get your tanks off my lawn."
- **The current Labour Cabinet.** One agreeable little quirk of the referendum campaign is that many of those running the country today were the young political anoraks who cut their political teeth on it. Even more enjoyable is that the oh-so-mainstream besuited bores of 2005 were anti-marketeer firebrands in 1975, and one hopes that they are suitably humble and realistic about their youthful fallibility, but one imagines not. So we find, for example, Jack Straw, memorably described in Benn's diaries as "a young lawyer on the make", working as an advisor for Barbara Castle. Straw, in a previous incarnation as President of the National Union of Students, had as early as 1969 been attacked by Enoch Powell, on whose side he was now working. The aforementioned Secretary of State for International Development, the impeccably New Labour Hilary Benn (eerily similar in manner to his father), was also involved, seconded from the ASTMS research department to work with GBO in the offices of the right wing magazine *The Spectator*. For some reason, involvement of the current generation of Tories in the campaign is harder to trace.

Opinion

So much for the personalities. How were they perceived by the public?

Table 5, had it been compiled in 1975, should have given the NRC pause for thought. The average madness quotient is over three, even though the figures are skewed by the deeply ordinary Jack Jones and Peter Shore. Being odd in politics, for an individual, can be very useful in establishing an identity; in this list it is the loonier ones who are most recognised. But *en masse* a group of odd people is off-putting; recall, as one example, the effect of John Redwood's launching his bid for the leadership of the Tory Party in 1995 against a backdrop of strange supporters in brightly coloured clothes.

And look at the approval rating column. All but two are negative. Powell had a positive rating, and indeed was liked and respected by one person in three — but because he polarised opinion so much his negative rating was almost equally high. Peter Shore had the opposite problem: 55% of people didn't know who he was, and 28% had no particular feelings about him. For the others, the negativity of their approval ratings was ominous, Ian Paisley's in particular.

The no camp appeared to the public of the time to consist of a load of mad, unpopular weirdos. This did not bode well for the campaign.

Table 5: Public Attitudes to Leading Figures in the No Camp*

Politician	Person known	Respect and like	Don't like	Approval rating	Good points	Bad points	Interesting?	Mad?
Enoch Powell	92%	33%	31%	+2	Brilliant	Pandering to race prejudice	5	5
Ian Paisley	83	3	62	-59	None	Bigoted	5	5
Tony Benn	81	17	32	-15	Earnest	Suspected by surprisingly many people of plotting the overthrow of the United Kingdom	4	5
Michael Foot	79	17	26	-9	Intellectual	Too left wing	5	3
Hugh Scanlon	75	13	30	-17	Effective	Over-mighty	2	2
Jack Jones	74	17	22	-5	Ordinary	Too powerful	1	1
Clive Jenkins	74	18	25	-7	Witty	Arrogant	4	3
Peter Shore	45	10	7	+3	Inoffensive	Unknown	1	1

* Also taken from Butler & Kitzinger. Barbara Castle, inexplicably, was excluded from the original Harris survey. It is quite possible that her ratings would have been much more positive than the average no campaigner.

Chapter Seven

The Campaign

Labour's Special Conference

The opening skirmishes of the campaign took place entirely within the labyrinthine structures of the Labour Party, pitting party man against party man. With the Tories, the Liberals and all the newspapers except the *Morning Star* in the yes camp, the no camp really needed Labour to come out against if it was to have any firm organisational backing at all.

On the other hand the no camp was as hamstrung as the Wilson leadership—neither wished to split the party in two. The noes had lined up seven members of the cabinet and thirty junior ministers, and by the time the renegotiations were coming to a close, a majority of the Parliamentary Labour Party; the Government's majority in the house on matters European was being preserved by opposition votes. With the membership assumed to be anti as well, a special party conference was called at the end of April, to try to bring all sides to bear on the leadership, and to recommend rejection of the renegotiated terms.

On March 26th, the National Executive Committee (representative of the broad membership of the party) had recommended a 'no' vote, in direct contradiction of Government policy—despite Wilson and Callaghan sitting on the NEC. But then the initiative collapsed into wrangling. A huge policy statement to be released at the special conference under the NEC's name was commissioned and presented to the next NEC meeting on April 23rd, but Callaghan wrecked it by proposing an impossible 300 amendments. In the end the messages were mixed: the document was released without NEC endorsement, together with a Government statement putting its own view.

With Labour's activists in full cry, and feelings running high at the conference, the NEC motion urging a 'no' vote was carried by 3.75 million votes to 2m. But that didn't settle the matter. There was no doubt that the party had overwhelmingly rejected the EEC. But did that mean the Labour Party organisation, in Parliament, through the unions, and in the country, would be at the disposal of the no camp in the forthcoming referendum? Were we to be treated to the delicious spectacle of a Labour Government initiative supported by the opposition parties, and opposed by the Labour Party? The party organisation was in the hands of the NEC, so the conference resolution meant yet another special meeting, this time of the NEC on 1st May, called by anti-marketeers hoping for exactly that outcome.

But between the special conference and the NEC meeting, somehow the no camp was outflanked. Wilson and Callaghan were absent, carousing with Commonwealth leaders in Jamaica, but their long arms managed to stitch up proceedings. General Secretary Ron Hayward announced that after two general elections the previous year the party's coffers were bare, and therefore no money would be released for a campaign.

The Labour anti-marketeers had no choice but to run their campaign through the National Referendum Campaign; they could not manage it from the left. This was an extraordinary way to run politics, but it is worth reminding ourselves that that is how we did it then. Anyhow, the shenanigans warmed everyone up. At about the same time, the content of the three officially-distributed pamphlets was leaked to the *Daily Telegraph*, and opposition politicians started to position themselves; Willie Whitelaw became the first to muse out loud about whether the referendum result could be ignored by Parliament, showing how nervous the yes camp remained; Britain in Europe hosted a big rally for the troops. We were off and rolling, with a month to polling day.

The First Week

The first week of campaigning, starting on Sunday 4th May, produced a touch of surrealism. Ignoring all the good arguments for membership, Edward Heath gave us a bad one: the red menace. It was the communists who wanted Britain out. This does rather overlook the possibility that the communists might be right; surely there were more telling points to be made. For the noes, Tory MP Neil Marten replied neatly that fourteen million voters within the EEC had voted communist at their last national elections, whereas in the UK the comparable figure was 17,000. Which communists was Heath referring to?

At this stage the war was phoney. Although ministers were warned not to make statements contravening Government policy in the Commons, and although one discontented industry minister, Eric Heffer, had been sacked for doing just that, Peter Shore made a mischievous intervention that managed to convey his opposition to the EEC without actually putting it into words. And at a meeting of the National Economic Development Board, yet another of the committees that drove industrial policy in those days of *corporativismo*, Benn had poked fun at Shirley Williams by raising the idea that Britain in Europe was the first stage of an all-party coalition government (a potential development that he had discussed in private with Shore over a year earlier).

All good knockabout stuff, but while Benn was teasing Williams, Wilson, pina colada in hand in his Jamaican hotel, was taking the gloves off. Not only did he manage to discomfit the no camp by persuading the Commonwealth leaders to endorse British membership of the EEC (neatly skewering the left on their own sentimental attachment to the Commonwealth), but he also leaked his plans to move Benn in a post-referendum reshuffle, the first major blow in an uncoordinated but deliberate series of *ad hominem* attacks on the strange and maladjusted figures that made up the no camp. 'Sack Benn' was the *Sun*'s headline on the 9th, and the *Daily Mirror* led with 'Bennmania'. Benn himself was getting the shock of his life—having assumed that student = radical = anti-EEC, he found himself addressing a markedly pro-Europe audience at Bristol University.

By the end of the week, as the feeling spread that the country was going to hell in a handcart—on May 9th, Environment Secretary Anthony Crosland was warning free-spending local authorities that "the party's over"—patriotic and celebratory notes were being sounded. BIE held the first of what proved to be a series of nightly rallies around the country, while for the NRC Enoch Powell was trusting to the good sense of the British people and the democratic power of public argument to keep Britain clear of 'political hobgoblins'.

The Second Week

The Sunday papers on the 11th were still fixating on Benn's war with Wilson. Two of them even carried the same headline: 'Bye Bye Benn'. Eric Heffer, brow furrowed, opened up a fertile new front for the anti-marketeers, muttering about his former ministerial colleagues coordinating with the European Commission. It was Heath's turn to wrap himself in the Union Jack, accusing the anti-marketeers of thinking the Britain was too weak to prosper *within* the EEC. Britain, meanwhile, seemed too weak to prosper anywhere: the Bank of England had to step in to halt a run on the pound.

Those organising the campaigns were mainly worried about boring the pants off everyone, and it was only now that the regular press conferences began, the NRC's first on 12th May, and BIE's on the 13th. As per usual, BIE excelled in oneupmanship—not once, but twice. The NRC managed to mess up their first conference by putting forward some unknown lawyers to develop a complex, doubtless important, but sadly tedious argument about the loss of sovereignty. While BIE nabbed the 10.45 timeslot, which got them the juiciest positions on the lunchtime TV news as well as baggsing the headlines in the *Evening Standard*.

The radicals were still unsuccessfully courting students. On the 13th, the anti-establishment Get Britain Out campaign managed to bomb by attempting a joint press conference with the National Union of Students. One of the students seemed not to be, as he maintained, a late 'no' convert, while another revealed a pro-Europe t-shirt. Meat and drink to Reg Prentice, who carried on with BIE's attacks on the madmen in the no camp ("the way-out factions: the Tribune group, the Communist Party, the Powellites, the National Front"; for some reason he forebore to include members of the Cabinet in which he served). In the House of Commons the next day, Tony Benn went where Reg had feared to tread, accusing not only the Tories on the benches opposite but also "present Cabinet ministers" of "a hatred of working people".

Remarks like that made it inevitable that the campaign would continue to focus, as Benn feared, on personalities not issues, though one might wonder why he continued to act in such a way as to make his personality an issue. Everyone piled in; Wilson called Benn a "beardless Old Testament prophet", while David Steel called him "Mr Phoney Benn".

The constitutional issues were aired by both sides, Michael Foot claiming that association with the EEC would suck Britain into the coalition way of doing things, while Margaret Thatcher developed Whitelaw's thought that Parliament could ignore the referendum altogether. And bullish patriotism, once more in the shape of Enoch Powell, found itself competing for headlines with disastrous economic news, as inflation leapt to 30% (that's not a misprint, 21st century reader, thirty per cent; these were the good old days).

The Third Week

By the beginning of the third week of the campaign, it was clear that the main issue wasn't sovereignty, or prices, or defence, or international relations, or high finance. It was Tony Benn. The yes camp's low-risk strategy of glossing over the issues was paying off. As for the polls, they weren't moving at all; the big lead for a 'yes' vote that had appeared when the government had made its recommendation remained. To that extent, the campaign was either a waste or time, or a stalemate.

But some in the yes camp began to fear that the risks of continued personal attacks on Benn were beginning to outweigh the benefits. With the traditional British belief in fair play still extant in these pre-Thatcher years, the pro-Europeans didn't want to gift sympathy votes to the noes. It was tacitly decided to back away from the attacks on Benn.

But that strategy was always doomed. Benn chose the one moment when he could have receded from the spotlight by making his most contentious claim: that membership of the EEC had already cost Britain half a million jobs. The argument had merit, based on deflation and the shift to a trade deficit over the previous couple of years, although it made a number of contentious assumptions. Benn certainly made a serious effort to shift the debate from personalities, but in doing so put forward such a crude caricature of a complex argument as to raise doubts whether the direct democracy he favoured could possibly host the detailed forensic examination that such claims merited. Half a million was the number of the week, as the Intervention Board also admitted that that was the number of tons of milk powder the EEC had stockpiled, so at least each of Benn's unemployed could have a ton of it.

Meanwhile, the media were beginning to stretch, yawn and take an interest. Two of the biggest brains in the campaign, Enoch Powell and Shirley Williams, met head to head on *Panorama* on the Monday, while on Tuesday Robin Day began a series of phone-in programmes. The Benn row rumbled on, with Wilson chipping in in Parliament on Tuesday disputing the unemployment claim. The *Daily Telegraph*'s referendum page piled on the pressure: 'Benn Factor Now Dominant Issue in Campaign'. The European Commission helpfully threw in a £15m loan to a steel mill in Michael Foot's constituency.

Wednesday 21st saw Giscard d'Estaing thinking aloud: maybe the EEC could move forward to economic and monetary union without the struggling economies of Britain and Italy. Benn immediately came back by pointing out that this would produce a two-tier community, a 'rich man's club' where the laggards should be grateful for whatever pickings were available. Thursday saw another rebuttal of Benn's unemployment argument, this time from Chief Whip Bob Mellish who detected "doubtful logic and raging fantasy"; at the same time the real unemployment figures were up, to what—at that time—seemed the dizzy heights of 817,000.

The campaigns were starting to communicate directly to voters, rather than through media intermediaries. After a printers' go-slow, individual leaflets were starting to get through. The distribution of the official pamphlets began, as did the TV broadcasts, and the yes camp's strategy of producing comforting images and glossing over argument continued to produce results, while the no camp's opposite strategy of making arguments and soft-pedalling on presentation made no headway. The yes camp imported an expensive American propagandist, Charles Guggenheim, who had worked on the (disastrous) Presidential campaign of George McGovern in 1972; he produced a series of films designed to give the viewer a warm, fuzzy feeling about the EEC. Ordinary people, in their own context, chatted to leading BIE campaigners. In contrast, the antis had cheap, newsy discussions on selected topics. BIE spent forty-two times as much as the NRC on broadcasts; you needn't wonder which were the more successful—and of course all BIE had to do was achieve parity, such was their lead in the polls. On the other hand, many of BIE supporters disliked the American slickness of the broadcasts, feeling that they shifted attention away from the ideas they were campaigning for.

The Wilson-Benn feud rumbled on. On Friday 23rd, Wilson announced a rescue plan for the British textile industry in the Commons, under the stewardship, not of Secretary of State for Industry Benn, but rather the Chancellor of the Duchy of Lancaster Harold Lever. Benn was pointedly absent. But on the same day, Wilson tentatively opened the door to a more robust campaign by relaxing the strict guidelines governing Cabinet members. Crucially, Cabinet ministers could now appear together in opposition on the same programme. The media salivated about Benn v Jenkins.

To close the week, another intervention from outside—American President Gerald Ford reiterated America's long-held view that Britain should be a big player in Europe—and further pondering about coalitions as the way to deal with Britain's long-term decline, this time from George Brown. The Chairman of the Indian Workers Association argued that non-white people would move from being second class citizens in Britain to third class citizens in the EEC, but the combined presence in the no camp of the radical left and the Powellite anti-immigration right made it hard for them to follow through this line of thought. The polls refused to budge.

The Fourth Week

Although there was under a fortnight to go, there was little passion in the fourth week of campaigning, although it got off to a flying start as the National Front tried to disrupt Ted Heath's speech in Glasgow. After the weekend lull, familiar themes were reheated. Reggie Maudling was the latest Tory to write about the referendum's being advisory, not binding, in a letter in the *Times*. Peter Shore gave the latest patriotic 'no' speech, while Ted Heath pointed out that if Britain got a reputation for tearing up treaties it had signed, it might end up with no treaties at all. BIE chose the bank holiday Monday to risk allowing its youth group to host a press conference; with few journalists in attendance it passed without disaster, although another current member of the Blair Cabinet, Peter Hain, complained that BIE had censored his radical speech.

Bennmania continued apace. Chancellor of the Exchequer Denis Healey, who, having problems of his own, had kept a deliberately low profile popped up on Sunday 25th to chunter about how truth had been a casualty of the campaign, with one eye on Benn's unemployment claims. Benn, unabashed, repeated them next day, while his Parliamentary Under-Secretary Michael Meacher even added a further 200,000 to the figure in a speech on Wednesday. Roy Jenkins had fun with a widely-quoted observation that he found it "increasingly difficult to take Mr Benn seriously as an economics minister".

Benn's riposte was to use his slot on Robin Day's phone-in to do the personalities/issues thing: "What you are being asked to decide is whether you want Britain to be self-governing and independent, or whether you want to be under Commissioners you cannot remove," which was certainly an admirably precise statement of the issue at hand. Nevertheless, there were two further considerations that Benn didn't follow up. First, there was the additional question of whether Britain might be better off under bureaucratic rule from Brussels as opposed to what appeared to be helpless and hopeless British politicians, be they ever so removable. After all, Heath's Government had been removed, and replaced with Wilson's (which had, in 1970, itself been replaced), with no great improvement. Sovereignty is all very well, but it butters no parsnips. And secondly, there was an increasing sense among many sectors of Britain's population that what they really wanted to do was to get rid of Benn and the unions, but all the sovereignty in the world seemed incapable to achieving that in 1975.

Much of the campaign had involved the two camps talking past each other, and genuine confrontations were at a premium. One of the silliest happened round about this time, and as usual it was BIE who got the upper hand. Barbara Castle had made much of higher food prices thanks to the CAP, and to prove her point she flew to Brussels, buying a basket of food for £6.92 that had cost her £4.24 back in Blighty. But her *coup* leaked, and when she came to announce the discovery at a press conference on the 29th, BIE were able to exhibit goods to the value of £5.82 in Britain that had cost a whopping £10.05 in Norway. This 72% rise was attributed (by BIE) to the costs of keeping Norway *out* of the union. Of course, this was technically a very inchoate argument: all that had been proved was that Britain was cheaper than anywhere, in or out of the market, and you could put this down, as you preferred, to Britain's membership of the EEC for the last two years, or its non-membership in the preceding fifteen.

The Commission outdid themselves. Earlier in the week they had continued their don't-worry-we're-not-taking-sides-at-all aid to the yes camp by doling out £42m of loans to British industry, as well as making a well-timed announcement that since joining Britain had received £210m of food subsidies from Brussels. But then they showed some previously unsuspected tactical nous. Benn had developed a plan to save the hopeless car company British Leyland (effectively by lobbing wads of dosh at it in the hope that some would stick), which he suspected contravened EEC regulations, and had been accusing the Commission of delaying their veto announcement until after the referendum. Instead, the Commission announced their *support* of the plan on May 29th, and wind was taken from Benn's sails. Needless to say, such good sense lasted round about 24 hours; on the 30th, Danish Commissioner Finn Gundelach made a speech in Glasgow criticising Benn's "horribly naïve concept of the world economy", a criticism that may indeed have been true but whose airing showed an impressive lack of political skills.

Harold Wilson ended the week with a bit of good news for the NRC. His pointed restatement of the temporary nature of the relaxation of collective responsibility for the purposes of the campaign was seen as a sideswipe at Jenkins rather than Benn, who had very rarely let personal animus drive his contributions.

The Fifth Week

June was upon us, and the campaign was starting to warm up. BIE wisely dampened down reports that the European Commission would not be satisfied with less than a 60% 'yes' vote in the referendum. Since the main enemies by now were complacency or some disastrous unpredictable breakdown, this was the last intervention they wanted. Neither did anyone really want Reg Prentice raising the issue of a coalition government during this time of British economic travail—though he unhelpfully did. Risk aversion was the order of the day.

The NRC was in trouble, and struggling. Powell moved away from patriotism with a blistering anti-establishment article in the *News of the World*, while an obscure left wing Labour MP walked out on Wilson during a meeting and demanded that he be disciplined for going against the NEC's line. Perhaps the one bright spot of the last weekend before polling was that the relatively sensible Scottish Secretary, Willie Ross, made his one contribution to the anti-EEC campaign. Unusually conscious of the collateral damage that the referendum could cause the Labour Party, he had tried to avoid actions that might boost the Scottish National Party in Scotland.

The TV coverage stepped up. *Weekend World* ran a special on Sunday night, while Granada showed *State of the Nation* the next day, a debate between Heath, Jenkins, Maudling, Roy Hattersley, David Steel and Tory MEP John Davies for the yeses, opposed by Powell, Shore, Douglas Jay, Marten, Labour minister Judith Hart and SNP MP Douglas Henderson. Hart replaced Tony Benn at the last minute; Benn had always refused to share a platform with non-Labour antis, and although Granada offered him no fewer than seven possible seating arrangements to keep him away from the contamination of Powell, Marten or Henderson, he couldn't agree to join the debate. It was generally agreed that Peter Shore had shone most brightly.

Panorama was able to broadcast what everyone had wanted to see: Benn v Jenkins. But the two were much more polite in person than they had been in the privacy of their own press conferences, and they settled down for a good discussion centring mostly around Benn's half million lost jobs. The result was more or less a draw; Benn recorded relief in his diary that he had done well, but with only three days to go he really needed a knockout. Also on the 2nd June, we had a blast from the past: the leader of the first attempt to join the EEC, Harold Macmillan, came out of retirement to do one more turn for Britain's membership.

On June 3rd, with two days to go, the Tories briefly took over. At a press conference, Thatcher tried to defend herself against charges of a lukewarm campaign with a powerful intervention in favour of membership, but she was upstaged in the news later when the Chairman of the 1922 Committee of backbench Tory MPs, Edward du Cann (a devoted Machiavellian who had been credited with organising the deposition of Ted Heath, earning himself the soubriquet 'du Cann of worms') claimed that at least half the Tory Party was anti-market. This was something of a surprise, as it was generally thought that, as one of the Tories' 'men in grey suits', du Cann should know what he was talking about. And as a 20th century Machiavel, it was also assumed that du Cann was up to something unspeakably sly. However, no-one worked out what that thing could be, and it turned out, once the results of the referendum had been analysed, that du Cann actually *didn't* know what he was talking about. A backbencher called for a vote of no confidence in him, but he sailed through the next election for Chairman of the 1922 with no opposition. Nevertheless, a mysterious incident.

At the NRC, Enoch Powell enjoyed himself with a vicious and humorous press conference attacking Heath. "I would dearly have liked to be friends with Ted," said he, "but, like everyone else, I found it impossible." Benn, in the face of bookies' odds of 1/8 for a yes vote, claimed that things were moving in his direction.

For referendum fans there was a feast on the telly that night. The George Brown-Clive Jenkins coach trip round Europe entertained 8.9m viewers on *World in Action*, while the Beeb showed a debate at the Oxford Union with Thorpe and Heath proposing the motion, Castle and Shore opposing. Once more Shore was on tip-top form, while Heath, somewhat late in the day, chipped in with the passionate defence of the sacrifice of sovereignty that many in the yes camp had wanted a long time ago. 10.8m watched.

One day to go: June 4th. The *Sun* summed up the campaign for many, as a columnist headed his piece 'Wedgie[1] has decided me—I'm going to vote yes'. It was in the interests of both sides to play up the chances of the no camp winning, since certainty about the result would be the force most likely to keep voters at home.

[1] I.e. Tony (Anthony Wedgwood) Benn.

Hence both Christopher Frere-Smith (of GBO) and Neil Marten (of the NRC) followed Benn in detecting movement towards a no vote, while Jenkins warned that a low turnout would play into the anti-Europeans' hands, either by allowing them to win, or depriving the result of legitimacy. Prominent Liberal MP John Pardoe made an even stronger pitch for a federal Europe than Heath's TV performance, and complained about the failure of BIE to sell the European dream. "They have never once given even a glimmer of the glory of the European feast," quoth he, hinting that the clever PR men behind the campaign had really hamstrung it. Enoch Powell, meanwhile, seemed to have given up campaigning altogether and was now going back to his favourite sport of taunting Ted; he gave his final speech of the campaign from Heath's constituency. His other old enemy, Macmillan, turned up at BIE's final act, a torchlight vigil by Churchill's statue in Parliament Square.

Overview

A shapeless campaign (as it has been called)? Well, not really. Several themes emerged during the course of it, but what really stands out is the successful demonisation of Tony Benn. Enoch Powell was strangely subdued, a surprise indeed given the venom with which he was laying into Heath only fifteen months earlier. Neither did Barbara Castle or Michael Foot make much of an impact. Perhaps the most impressive performer in the no camp was Peter Shore, who was only given opportunity to shine in the last few days before polling.

Key arguments included: the question of whether Britain was strong enough to survive outside (or indeed within) the EEC, which quickly turned into a display of patriotism whenever the argument was made; the role of the European Commission in helping out the yes camp; the role of a referendum in a Parliamentary system, and whether it could ever be binding; the question of whether the centrist grouping of Britain in Europe was paving the way for a coalition. None of these, save perhaps the first, actually had very much to do with what were supposedly the issues. Even the patriotic first argument was really irrelevant, since the bad economic news with which Britain was awash, and which continued to trickle in during the campaign, meant that everyone knew that the country was a basket case. On the other hand, who could doubt that an industrial country of fifty million people would survive perfectly well within the community or without? The only relevant debates were those about prices (sparked by Castle's shopping trip to Brussels) and jobs (sparked by Benn's claim of the lost half million), and neither was decisive.

The polls stayed put—indeed, finer-grained polls than the usual yes/no questions also showed remarkable stability throughout the month of May. Was there much of a point to the whole thing? Well, it had happened; all that now remained was for everyone to put their crosses next to their preferred vision of the future.

Chapter Eight

The Results

As Expected

The final poll, a TV exit poll, gave the yes camp 68.3%, a colossal victory. Because of the odd rules for the count, counting proper did not start until the next morning, June 6th; the votes having been taken and amalgamated at county or regional headquarters overnight. The first result came from the Scilly Isles, Harold and Mary Wilson's beloved holiday home. Whether or not Wilson's presence helped, the result was certainly overwhelming: 74.5% yes. The first Welsh result, in Gwynedd, came shortly afterwards, and although a high no vote was anticipated, the yeses got 70.6%. The landslide was going to happen as expected.

Out of an electorate of a little over 40m, 26m voted, a decent 65% turnout. Admittedly that was less than the two recent general elections: February 1974 managed 78.7%, and October 1974 72.8%. But this was the third national ballot in sixteen months, and election fatigue had to be a factor. It was also a very boring topic, of interest only to the politically aware. And unlike the 1974 elections, the outcome seemed predestined; it was not an exciting vote. From our 21st century perspective, our young, smiling, besuited, managementspeaking politicians, with their focus groups and finely-honed psephology, would kill to have the 65% turnout produced by the middle-aged, shabby, unappealing, ideologically extreme class warriors of 30 years ago. There is no doubt that the turnout was respectable and the vote legitimate.

The result was very slightly closer than the exit poll predicted: 17,378,581 yes, 67.2%, 8,470,073 no, 32.8%. A massacre: the fullhearted approval that Heath had promised and Powell demanded.

England was most in favour. Turnout was about 65%, with bigger turnouts further South. Enthusiasm for the referendum seemed geographically correlated with enthusiasm for the EEC: 71.6% of Southerners voted yes, as opposed to 67.4% voting yes in the North. Most of the very big yes votes, Surrey, West Sussex, East Sussex, were in the South, though North Yorkshire bucked the trend and nabbed the highest. Tyne & Wear, at 62.9%, had the smallest yes percentage in England. London's, on 66.7%, was below average. But the regional variations were small, and the English result pretty uniform. The final yes tally in England was 68.7%.

England on its own would have decided the referendum, as the nationalists hoped. This in itself should give us pause when we think about the referendum as a device for making decisions in the British context. Of course there is nothing underhanded in the rules: if England votes, by a large majority, for a measure, then that means *ipso facto* that barring extraordinary results from elsewhere, more Britons would have voted for that measure than not. All well and good. Except that in this particular context, where the interests of three other home nations need to be balanced in a tricky constitutional tightrope act — a tightrope buffeted by the winds of gradual and permanent constitutional evolution — it is as important that England is seen not to dominate as it is for the Celtic tail not to wag the British dog.

As it was, this referendum put no pressure on the union. The other home nations surprised commentators and nationalists alike by voting yes along with England. 66.5% of the Welsh voted yes on a 66.7% turnout. Only the highly-populated Labour heartlands, the mining counties of the South, were relatively unenthusiastic, although even they all had clear yes majorities. Mid Glamorgan's yes vote, at 56.9%, was one of the lowest in Britain; Gwent and West Glamorgan also were comparatively low. Powys, in contrast, voted yes by a majority of three to one.

Scotland produced a sulky yes of 58.4%, on a lowish turnout of 61.7%. Only the Border region produced a yes vote in excess of 70%, which was put down to the presence locally of popular MP and prominent yes man David Steel. Otherwise, most regions had yes votes in the high 50s. However, Scotland did produce the only negative results, two of them, in two of the three smallest regions. The Shetlands produced a no vote of 56.3%, while in the Western Isles the noes got a whopping 70.1%. These two also produced two of the lowest turnouts, with under half of the Shetlanders braving the weather. Finally Northern Ireland, whose vote wasn't broken down into counties, was least enthusiastic of all home nations, with a 52.1% yes vote on a 47.4% turnout. The victory was resounding.

Finally, what of the unfortunate MPs whose constituencies exactly coincided with regional boundaries? Recall from Chapter Four that these alone could see exactly how their constituency voted, and therefore it could be seen exactly how in touch with their constituencies they were. How appalling it is that it might be made public knowledge that an MP's opinions diverged from those of his or her constituents! Anyway, the results, happily, vindicated the unfairly exposed three. The SNP MP for the Western Isles, Donald Stewart, got his no vote, while Stephen Ross saw the Isle of Wight produce a 70.2% yes. The other Liberal yes campaigner Jo Grimond, in Orkney and Shetland, managed a narrow majority when the scores from the (yes-voting) Orkneys and the (no-voting) Shetlands were added together. So that was all right then.

Reaction

Having produced an overwhelming endorsement of the status quo, in a world where the strategic and economic situation was anything but happy, the referendum was totally forgotten by June 7th, and almost never mentioned again. More pressing matters were pursued.

The principled no campaigners accepted the result with varying levels of phlegm. Tony Benn immediately agreed that the majority was overwhelming and the result decisive. In the privacy of his diaries, however, some resentment shows through: he complains that even with all three party leaders and virtually the whole of the press pushing for a yes vote, only 43% of the electorate actually so voted: this is not, he says, wholehearted consent. On the other hand, it might be pointed out in return, only 21% voted no.

At the NRC party on 6th June, Benn and Powell actually spoke for the first time for several years; Powell remained defiant. On Benn's account, Powell complained that the campaign was too quick, and that people were only just beginning to understand the issues. In an article a few days later, Powell deployed his characteristic logic of romance. "Never again, by the necessity of an axiom, will an Englishman live for his country or die for his country: the country for which people live and die was obsolete and we have abolished it." Only in one sense of the word did Powell 'accept' the result. Neil Marten was resigned, Clive Jenkins defiant.

The press welcomed the result, and Wilson got unusually good coverage. Some of the right wing papers gave the triumph to Heath, who needed some good news after a lousy couple of years.

After the dust had settled, the big question was how Wilson would reshuffle his Cabinet in the aftermath of the divisive campaign. Benn's diaries for early June 1975 speak of frantic damage limitation, calling in of favours, tears, speedy calculations of how to stand up to Wilson. Benn thought, and wrote, much in those few days about the disconnection between the Labour government and the Labour movement, rationalising his isolated position. But the referendum had boosted Wilson's credit at a time when his Parliamentary majority was precarious. He moved to strengthen his hand in the Cabinet with a minor reshuffle. The axe didn't fall exclusively on the anti-Europeans: Reg Prentice was sacked, possibly for his many pro-coalition comments during the campaign. But the most eye-catching move was the demotion of the industrious, energetic Benn from Industry to Energy, a personal blow, if an expected one. The move was particularly hard for Benn as he was piloting a large and difficult Industry Bill through the House at the time, and he thought long and hard about whether to resign.

Government continued. But the decisiveness of the victory meant that the membership question appeared to have been settled for the foreseeable future, so hedging of bets ceased. The Labour Party in particular had been ambivalent, and had boycotted the European Parliament since it was set up; now they sent their delegation. The TUC also for the first time took up the places on EEC institutions to which they were entitled. Government ministers could work with their European counterparts knowing that decisions taken now would indeed be binding in the future.

Ultimately there is no doubt as to the real loser of the 1975 referendum. The Rolls-Royce brain and Hillman Imp judgement of Enoch Powell had taken him a long way in a wilfully perverse political career. He is remembered for his notorious immigration policies, but his political speeches are as fine as anyone's. Many of the economic or foreign and defence policy arguments he produced in the 1960s were twenty years ahead of their time; his analysis of Vietnam deadly accurate.

He made the anti-EEC case within the Tory Party for six years after his sacking by Heath. He failed to persuade his colleagues to abandon their traditional loyalty, even though many were worried by Heath's poor leadership, u-turns and ideological impurity. Had Powell been returned as a Tory MP in February 1974, there is a good chance that he, not Margaret Thatcher, would have been able to launch a successful *coup*. Reverse history, though, is futile. What actually happened, in the week before the first 1974 election, is that Powell quit the Tory Party and recommended a Labour vote in order to get a referendum. Be careful what you wish for.

By October he was back in Parliament, but in Northern Ireland, the only Unionist who supported rule of Ulster from Westminster, a political giant surrounded by pygmies. The referendum had been a beautiful national stage on which he could strut, but a constitutional rarity. Even then, during the campaign he was eclipsed by Tony Benn. Afterwards, he was a politician in exile, and in isolation in his exile. Though he continued to make the occasional splash, his serious career was, to all intents and purposes, over.

A Great Triumph for Direct Democracy, and Yet ...

The result was clear and resounding. But entirely satisfactory? That's a different matter. Let's round off this chapter with a brief checklist of worries about the 1975 referendum as a means of decision-making.

In the first place, the campaign pitted the entire establishment against a few mavericks. All the major parties and virtually all the national press lined up on one side; Benn, Powell, Foot and Castle were a small, and fatally disparate opposition, backed only by the *Morning Star*. This preponderance of opinion made it more difficult, not only for the no arguments to get a hearing, but also for them to be taken seriously. Nowadays it might be harder for establishment muscle to swing a vote; in France and Holland, mavericks have defeated a united establishment under similar circumstances in recent referendums and elections. But the 70s were somewhat more deferential in some, if not all, crucial respects. People went on strike more in the 70s, but they also took the opinion of their leaders more seriously. Opinion surveys show that voters are more cynical about politicians today.

Let us also distinguish between the Government and the establishment. That the establishment was in favour meant all the major politicians and all the press were urging a yes vote. Because EEC membership was Government policy as well, the neutrality of the civil service was undermined. The NRC, for example, complained about the bias of the Government's own information unit, but the civil servants were on a hiding to nothing. Perhaps the most egregious effect of the lack of Government neutrality was the production of a second pro-membership pamphlet by the Government (twice as long as the pamphlets of the two campaigning groups).

Furthermore the EEC itself was in favour of the continuation of British membership, having been a party to the renegotiation, and with just as much of a stake as Wilson in seeing the terms accepted. The campaign was punctuated by helpful loans, announcements and speeches emanating from Europe. The establishment, the Government and the European Commission were not wrong to do as they did, but together they constituted a powerful force for persuasion against a patently inadequate opposition.

Secondly, Chapters Five and Six show that not only were the two teams hopelessly uneven numerically, but also the prominent members of the no camp were deeply unpopular too. Tony Benn was a leading hate figure. Enoch Powell commanded vocal and loyal support, but had an equally vocal opposition too. Michael Foot was seen as a dangerous radical. Barbara Castle was associated with a number of unpopular, if sensible, innovations in transport. Ian Paisley was perceived as a loudmouthed bigot. Trade union support was unhelpful. One could have put together a more lurid rogues' gallery, but it would have been hard.

It might be said that, given that people trust politicians so much less than others, this disparity might not matter. Would not voters prefer to listen to church leaders, businessmen, academics and so on? They often tell pollsters that they would rather do so, and that they trust politicians' words less than other groups (except possibly journalists). This is no doubt true, but also irrelevant.

As Onora O'Neill argued in her Reith Lectures on trust, what people tell pollsters and what they actually do are different things. Much of the crisis of trust of the last few decades has been bravado in the costless response to abstract questions on a polling form. And Robert Worcester of MORI argues that anyway politicians are guaranteed a high profile in debates where the consensus is disputed. People may *want* to listen to businessmen or academics, and indeed television news programmes are more than willing to interview them. But where there are strict rules protecting broadcasters' balance, every interview with a pro-EEC businessman will be matched by one with an anti-EEC businessman, ditto academics, ditto churchmen, ditto celebrities. So, even if the weight of opinion among, say, business leaders was clear, a voice opposed to the consensus would have to be found and given an airing. No clear lead from any community would be available for voters other than from the politicians whose opinions and profiles are already relatively well-known. Hence it is the politicians whose messages, ironically, get over most easily, even though voters tell us that it is their messages in particular that they do not want to hear.

Thirdly, the no camp was much the less coherent of the two, both intellectually and as a political force. The yes camp looked strong and mutually self-supporting, and accepted more or less the same arguments. It consisted of the bulk of the Tory Party, plus the Liberals, plus the right of the Labour Party, in short a big chunk of people from the centre right, contiguously arrayed on the political spectrum. The no camp, on the other hand, was very diverse. Some worried about sovereignty, some worried about prices, others were keen to embarrass Wilson or the government, others fretted about a Papist plot. And the personnel didn't cohere either; the left of the Labour Party were added to nationalist conservatives on the right of the Tory Party who wished to retain the powers of Westminster, nationalists from Wales and Scotland who wished to erode the powers of Westminster, and politicians from all sides in Northern Ireland who interpreted EEC policies in mutually exclusive but exclusively demonising ways. Had there been a no vote by any chance, it is impossible that any clear rejectionist narrative could have been generated by what Benn had accurately characterised as an absolute rag-bag.

Fourthly, the terribly disparity of funds between the two camps is so obvious that it surely needs little further discussion. For instance, BIE spent £105,000 on making its four television broadcasts; the NRC spent £2,500. The NRC's broadcasts were more issues-focused than the more professional BIE pieces, but they lacked any conception of what would swing the target audience (or indeed what the target audience was). BIE had the funds to do the research and bring in expensive ad-men.

Fifthly, the organisation of the yes camp was much more professional, thanks partly to the funding advantage, partly to its access to the organisational capacity of campaigning organisations, and partly to the competence of its leading figures. The no camp contained too many organisations, and was too prone to infighting. It lacked an overarching strategy, and much of the unity it managed to display was thanks to the energy of its dedicated figurehead Neil Marten. In terms of the ability to get a message across, this was a serious handicap.

Sixthly, the yes camp broadly called the shots the moment that Britain joined. Referendums, it has been argued, are fundamentally conservative exercises; momentum and inertia count for more than

SOCIETAS
essays in political and cultural criticism

The Case Against the Democratic State
Gordon Graham

We are now so used to the state's pre-eminence in all things that few think to question it. This essay contends that the gross imbalance of power in the modern state is in need of justification, and that democracy simply masks this need with an illusion of popular sovereignty. Although the arguments are accessible to all, it is written within the European philosophical tradition. The author is Professor of Moral Philosophy at the Uniiversity of Aberdeen. 96 p., £8.95/$17.90

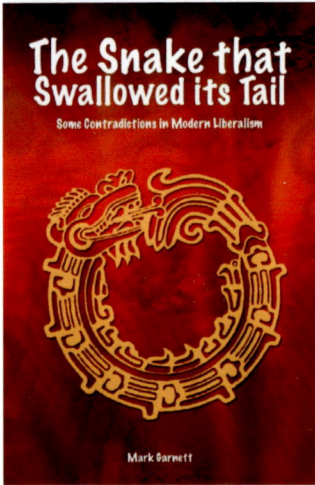

The Snake that Swallowed its Tail
Mark Garnett

Liberal values are the hallmark of a civilised society. Yet they depend on an optimistic view of the human condition, Stripped of this essential ingredient, liberalism has become a hollowed-out abstraction. Tracing its effects through the media, politics and the public services, the author argues that hollowed-out liberalism has helped to produce our present discontent. Unless we stop boasting about our values and try to recover their essence, liberal society will be crushed in the coils of its own contradictions. 96 pp., £8.95/$17.90

The Party's Over
Keith Sutherland

The book argues that the tyranny of the modern political party should be replaced by a mixed constitution in which advocacy is entrusted to an aristocracy of merit, and democratic representation is achieved via a jury-style lottery. 200 pp., £8.95/$17.90

- *'An extremely valuable contribution–a subversive and necessary read.'* **Graham Allen MP**, *Tribune*
- *'His analysis of what is wrong is superb . . . No one can read this book without realising that something radical, even revolutionary must be done.'* **Sir Richard Body**, *Salisbury Review*
- *'A political essay in the best tradition: shrewd, erudite, polemical, partisan, mischievous and highly topical.'* **Contemporary Political Theory**

ideas. It may be so; what is clear, when one looks at the polls, is that there was a strong possibility that a referendum conducted to legitimate initial negotiations with the EEC in 1971 might have been closer than the actual one, and might have had a different result. Once Britain was in, many were prepared to 'give Europe a chance'. But the referendum was only offered after the pro-Europeans had chosen the ground and the timing of the battle.

All these reasons, maybe more, entailed that the referendum wasn't a straightforward clash of ideas. Tony Benn was always in favour of discussions of policies, not personalities. Well, he didn't get one this time. The champions of membership were better prepared for the battle than their opponents. It may be that that preparedness is a symptom of the superiority of their beliefs. On the other hand, it might also be a contingent matter of no intellectual significance. Either way, the superior marshalling of the yes forces meant that the referendum had very little political effect; we would have seen more or less the same outcome had membership and ratification gone via the usual Parliamentary route.

Which makes one wonder what it was all *for*?

Chapter Nine

The Aftermath I

The European Question

Where Are We Now?

So the referendum was over. We have reviewed the event in some detail. The narrative, the theory, the rules, the finance, the organisation, the personalities, the result, all point towards a number of pretty basic conclusions: the whole thing was much more to do with politicians' immediate short-term needs; a major determinant of the result was the public perception of the leading campaigners; the trajectory of the decision-making process was determined by perceived threats and opportunities in Westminster, not by any great upsurge in demand for people power. Indeed, the public seemed on the whole rather uninterested in the affair, at least until campaigning reached a climax; the impressive turnout can't be used as an argument for a *pre*-existing desire on the voters' part to be consulted on this great constitutional issue.

It is extraordinary that the referendum, the greatest single-issue consultative exercise in British history, has not just receded but virtually disappeared from the national memory. Even people who voted in it have to be reminded that it happened. But an event as major as this, a striking deviation from the tacit principles of government that appear, ghost-like, in Britain's informal constitution, cannot be a storm in a teacup, and shouldn't be allowed to languish alongside other forgotten *causes célèbres* such as the Grunwick dispute or the petrol blockades.

Our final couple of chapters will examine the aftermath of the great debate of 1975. The use of a referendum to settle the issue of Europe prompts two questions. What happened to the issue? And what happened to the method of settling it? In the final chapter we will consider the latter, and review the post-1975 use of referendums in Britain. For now, our focus will be on the fraught history of the Common Market in British politics.

What Did We Vote For?

One argument made by Enoch Powell in the 1970 general election campaign was that a referendum question and debate could not be framed properly. If the terms were in doubt, then one couldn't vote responsibly because one wouldn't know exactly what membership entailed. If, on the other hand, the terms were known, then that would be the subject of a perfectly normal treaty which could only be amended properly if the government was defeated.

Overly influenced by unreliable opinion polls, Powell changed his mind about referendums. And anyway, the argument evaporated when Wilson formulated his policy: the new set of terms was decided *on the assumption* of their being put to the people. Is this an example of how a referendum could work when a government enters into commitments that entail constitutional upheaval? If we lay aside the standard arguments against the use of referendums in representative democracies for a moment, perhaps this is a textbook case of what a referendum is all about. A series of alternatives is set out, publicly debated, and evaluated by popular vote. Whether or not it is a welcome alternative to a parliamentary vote, whether or not the question is manipulated by political elites, whether or not financial resources are fairly distributed, surely the actual act of putting a proposal to the people, and letting them indicate a preference where it exists, for or against the proposal, is a perfectly coherent method of making a decision?

Not necessarily. Take the example of the single European currency. When the UK joined the EEC, the aim was to furnish Europe with a single currency by the end of the decade (i.e. 1980). Powell in particular fulminated against the folly of giving away control of monetary policy, so vital for governmental control of the economy. Britain had just gone through one monetary upheaval, with the replacement in 1971 of shillings and pence with new pence; that shift, which in theory made no difference economically (the pound was simply divided into 100 parts rather than 240), had been blamed for runaway inflation and a great deal of confusion. Few pro-Europeans anticipated popular support for another change; the single currency was hardly mentioned in the campaign.

Uncertainties soon crept in. 1973 brought the oil price shock, and severe global recession. As a result, many of the Community's favourite schemes and initiatives were put on hold. In December 1974, a meeting of the nine heads of the Common Market in Paris endorsed monetary union explicitly in a communiqué that was part of the package to be put to the British people, although Wilson repudiated the policy almost immediately in Cabinet. On March 17th 1975, in the Cabinet discussion over whether to recommend the renegotiated terms to the British people, there was still uncertainty, leading to an argument between Wilson and Michael Foot about whether monetary union was dead or not. If there was uncertainty between the Prime Minister and one of his most important ministers about the likelihood of a dramatic economic upheaval scheduled to happen in a mere five years' time, then how could an ordinary voter hope to make an informed decision? Monetary union was explicitly affirmed at the Paris meeting, and so explicitly was part of the renegotiated terms recommended in March, but Wilson—correctly as it turned out—argued that *de facto* there was no chance of it actually happening.

Indeed, much changed in that depressing decade that rendered assumptions and promises null and void. It had been assumed that agriculture would take up less and less of the community budget, and that industrial and regional policy would fill the gap as Europe's economy modernised. That was crucial for Britain, with its relatively efficient farmers and larger industrial sector. As it was, European agriculture became addicted to subsidies—rather than farmers turning up in Brussels cap in hand, it was the taxpayer who went to the farms CAP in hand—and the agriculture budget remains to this day unfeasibly high and ill-directed. Furthermore, no-one factored in Britain's dire economic performance in the late 70s, which made its contribution to the European budget much harder to bear than had been anticipated.

Seeing the future is a handy knack if you have it. Dealing with the unexpected under conditions of great uncertainty is part of the politician's job, and very hard it is too. No-one would seriously aver that, given a set of terms of a treaty, one could work out exactly how Britain would stand with respect to that treaty in five or ten or thirty years' time. This, perhaps, is a rather better version of Powell's argument about terms; if you fix the terms of membership, the context will change dramatically and the terms will become anachronistic and out of date, whereas if you allow flexibility in terms to adjust for uncertainty and changing contexts, then (as Powell argued) you can't put a firm question to the voters.

When Geoffrey Rippon's negotiations were complete, they were hailed as a triumph. In 1975, Jim Callaghan had renegotiated the terms, and produced an even better deal. But despite that, Margaret Thatcher still had to spend a great deal of time after her election in 1979 negotiating a further improvement in Britain's terms, eventually securing the famous rebate. Does that mean that Rippon or Callaghan had negotiated poorly, or settled too low? No — it means that the terms of a treaty are constantly evolving, and — again as Powell argued — that should make them subject to the nuanced analysis of the politician and continuous monitoring by Parliament, not the coarse-grained decision-making of a national election.

This is to argue neither that referendums are necessarily wrong, nor that voters make worse decisions than politicians, nor that voters make poor decisions. It is only that the presentation of an argument at a fixed point in time makes it hard to legislate for the dynamic aspects of a situation. By the time the British people went to vote for or against the renegotiated terms of British EEC membership, those terms were already obsolete *de facto*, as Harold Wilson had cannily maintained.

But on the other hand, what comes of the referendum result whenever the political context changes? It can't be that a new referendum is needed every time that happens. In that case, it has to be that the result has 'stickability', that its legitimacy is accepted across contexts. Did that happen after 1975?

Labour, Europe and the Social Democrats

In his *Britain Says Yes*, written without hindsight in the immediate aftermath of the referendum, Anthony King allows himself to speculate about what would have happened had there been a no vote; he suggests that the results would have been cataclysmic for the Government and the Labour Party, and furthermore would have precipitated economic disaster. The referendum didn't change history, but it did prevent history being changed. He reckons that Roy Jenkins and Shirley Williams would have quit, and the Government would have collapsed.

Doubtless a no vote would have provoked a crisis; that is not our focus here. But King's sanguine assumption about the consequences of the yes vote is, we now know, very wide of the mark. Despite the high turnout and walloping majority, the vote didn't 'put the issue to bed'. The no camp, with few exceptions, didn't accept that, in Benn's words, they were in receipt of a message from the British people, and the legitimacy of the result was brushed aside by many as soon as the more obvious wounds of defeat scabbed over.

Enoch Powell wrote at the time of the referendum that he was ashamed of his country, that referendum day had echoes of September 1938. He was on record as saying the significance of the referendum was not that it would "decide whether Britain is to be part of the Common Market or not. What it will decide is whether Britain ceases to be part of the Common Market now or somewhat later." In 1977, he opined that "I will not say that you need to travel as far in Britain to find someone who voted Yes in the referendum as in Germany to find someone who was a Nazi; but they are becoming fewer, and the number of those who admit that they were wrong is growing."

The Bennite left, which after the electoral defeat of 1979 made a concerted effort to take over the navigation of the Labour Party, made withdrawal from Europe one of the key planks of policy of the early 80s. The 1983 manifesto explicitly promised to pass the legislation to prepare for Britain's withdrawal from the EEC within the lifetime of the Parliament. Admittedly a commitment to prepare is not a commitment to withdraw, but even so, within eight years of the referendum that 'put the issue to bed' the issue appeared to be still up and around. Even in 1987, with no mention of withdrawal, the acceptance of the reality of EEC membership was no more than grudging.

It is an unexamined axiom of Labour Party watchers that the headcases are all on the left. Actually, the right is less likely to blink first. During the October 1974 election campaign, for example, Shirley Williams, sitting next to a startled Harold Wilson, had vowed to quit politics if Britain left the EEC. No pressure, Harold.

Even with a 'yes' vote in the bag Jenkins and Williams deliberately split the Labour Party, the only possible electoral vehicle for the left, hoping thereby to cripple it. The alert reader, with the benefit of hindsight, will have spotted a number of signals in the narrative. There was much discussion during the campaign of a new coalition of all the talents, jettisoning the Bennite and Powellite extremes, to deal with the crises of the day. Many people were surprised that the referendum did not become the platform for an assertive centre. Britain in Europe brought many of the chief moderates together to cooperate across party lines. When prominent, if somewhat off-message members of the Labour government such as Jenkins and Williams were routinely hob-nobbing with the likes of Willie Whitelaw and Reggie Maudling, John Whitehorn of the CBI and Vic Feather, formerly of the TUC, and clearly getting along better than they did with colleagues such as Tony Benn or Eric Heffer, or nominal supporters like Jack Jones and Hugh Scanlon, suspicions were raised that BIE looked like the nucleus of a centre-right party that could command the support of a good chunk of the electorate, and could fragment the opposition between left, right and the nationalists.

There is no doubt that most of the participants in BIE enjoyed the experience. But despite the trust that had built up between former antagonists, nothing tangible emerged immediately. However when we look at the Labour members prominent in the 1975 campaign, alongside Jenkins and Williams we find Bill Rodgers, Dickson Mabon, Tom McNally, John Roper, Tom Bradley and David Marquand, for instance. This is the nucleus of the Social Democratic Party, which broke away from the Labour Party in 1981. Indeed, the only member of the Gang of Four who signed the Limehouse Declaration in 1981 who has not featured in our story was David Owen, who though undoubtedly pro-European was much the most eurosceptic figure in the SDP.

BIE didn't morph into the SDP. The Liberals stayed at arm's length for as long as possible, and only merged with it from a position of greater strength when the SDP had been undermined by a resurgent Labour Party and poor leadership from the divisive Owen. Crucially the Tories left well alone, despite the ideological zeal of the Thatcher government deplored by many on the left of the party. Christopher Brocklebank-Fowler earned his footnote in history as the single Tory MP to defect to the SDP. No Whitelaw, no Heath, no Douglas Hurd, no Francis Pym, no Jim Prior, no Norman St John Stevas.

On the other hand, it does seem reasonable to suggest that the referendum widened fissures already present in the Labour Party. Both Benn and Jenkins were willing to countenance a political realignment of Britain. Benn welcomed Thatcher's election as Tory leader, as it would present the British people with real alternatives at the next election; Jenkins, after serving as the President of the European Commission, used his Dimbleby lecture to raise the possibility of "breaking the mould". By breaking with Labour, Jenkins et al hoped to leave a Bennite rump, but succeeded only in weakening the Labour Party and splitting the progressive vote, bequeathing Britain eighteen years of radical Tory government. In the end, the ideological realignment that both men wanted happened, but only thanks to hard work within the Labour Party itself, by (in their different ways) Neil Kinnock, John Smith and Tony Blair and their colleagues to marginalise Benn and his supporters. In doing so, the social democracy that Jenkins wanted to establish vanished; the result has been twenty-five years of politics centred around varying versions of Thatcherism. It is probably safe to say that that was not an outcome either Benn or Jenkins was fighting for.

Wilson organised and fought a referendum to prevent Labour's boil being lanced, and succeeded—but the poison remained intact, and it is hard to argue that the short-term benefit of keeping Labour in office for four grim years was worth the eighteen years in the wilderness, after which Labour were so hungry for power that relatively little remained of the policy programmes Wilson, Callaghan, Foot, Benn and even Jenkins supported.

Maastricht and the Tories

That is now ancient history. But the ripples of the referendum still lap against the shores of our immediate political consciousness; the wreckage of the Tory Party is still visible at low tide. The European Union, as it was renamed by the 1992 Maastricht Treaty, is the cause, in one way or another, of virtually all the Tories' travails for the last twenty years. The Westland Affair sparked off the feud between Thatcher and Michael Heseltine that created her assassin. Her increasingly strident anti-European tone alienated Nigel Lawson and Geoffrey Howe and left her isolated; it was Howe's pro-European resignation speech that finished her off. The Tories' reputation for economic competence was destroyed by the expensive failure to keep the pound in its trading band in the European Monetary System. The guerrilla campaign in Parliament against the Maastricht Treaty after 1992 made the party look like a shambles, while showing John Smith's Labour Party in an unusually favourable light. It also destroyed John Major's thin majority in the Commons. It was the pretext for the pointless leadership election in 1995. Kenneth Clarke, easily the best candidate for leader in 1997 and 2001, was disqualified each time by his Europhilia. William Hague's moderate Euroscepticism, backed by the clever slogan of 'In Europe but not run by Europe', warped under electoral pressure into a silly, shrill vote-losing campaign to save the pound. Iain Duncan Smith's past as a Maastricht rebel meant he was incapable of imposing a leader's authority on MPs. Even now, after the 2005 general election the

Tories are numerically further from government than Michael Foot's Labour Party in 1983.

The negotiation of the Maastricht Treaty in 1992 was hailed as a triumph for John Major. The Commons debate in the immediate aftermath of the negotiations passed the government's motion by 83 votes, with only seven Tory rebels. But opinion in the party quickly turned against it, as it became clearer that the treaty had turned the union into something more of a separate political entity. This came as a shock to many: "it wasn't what we voted for in 1975!" Even after the supposedly decisive referendum result, even after Thatcher's Single European Act, there was a hard body of Tory opinion that was unable to let the European question remain settled — despite the fact that it was one of the achievements of a Tory government! It was as if, bizarrely, the referendum could only be regarded as decisive if the EEC/EU remained in stasis, and didn't evolve with the international political and economic context, as if every time the conditions changed a new referendum was needed.

And, lest we forget, a small part of the Tories' downfall in 1997 was orchestrated by a single-issue party: James Goldsmith's Referendum Party wanted a referendum on the topic of whether Britain remained in the EU. One of the more disturbing, though less often recalled, images of election night 1997 was Goldsmith's leering jeering at defeated pro-European Tory David Mellor. Why Goldsmith thought that a referendum in 1997 would settle the matter any more than did the referendum in 1975 is a moot point. And such ideas occurred not only in the fevered brains of fringe weirdos like Goldsmith; seventy-eight Tory MPs voted for a bill introduced in Parliament in June 1996 by Bill Cash calling for a referendum on Britain's membership in the wake of the BSE crisis.

It is hard to imagine a clearer-cut result in any referendum about a contested matter, but if a 67% yes vote on a 65% turnout cannot settle an issue for more than a handful of years, perhaps we should come to accept that such consultative exercises are not serious attempts by politicians to refer tricky or important decisions to a higher body. They are part of the political landscape, framed by politicians, and when the political landscape changes, then so does the understood significance of a result.

Referendums in Europe

This appears to be true even in countries with stronger traditions of direct democracy, particularly in the context of the EU where a national referendum has important cross-border ramifications.

The Maastricht Treaty is an interesting case in point. In the UK it was a problem, but at least it was ratified by Parliament (if only when Major treated it as a confidence issue). But in Europe, it was very nearly a disaster. In two of the twelve member nations (Ireland and Denmark), referendums were compulsory. In France, President Mitterand called a referendum for political reasons of his own. Ireland's referendum went off all right, but the Danes rejected the treaty by 51–49 in June 1992. This plunged Europe into a crisis, and the French referendum suddenly became the crux: rejection by French voters would kill the treaty. As it was, the French just voted in favour, also by 51–49. However, an EC treaty has to be ratified by all member states, and the Danes had rejected it. So that was that, right?

Wrong! The Danes were told, in effect, to vote again, with a strong implication that they would have to keep voting until they agreed. 51-49 was too close to legitimise the result. That is a fair point, except that one then realises it was exactly the same margin as the French yes but no-one asked the French to vote again. The whole concept of legitimacy here was defined in terms of the political project of European leaders of the time. As in 1975, a lot of official time and resources had been spent on achieving a multilateral agreement, and, despite the supposed commitment to consult the people, it was not acceptable for such consultation to end in the agreement being thrown out—adjusted maybe, implementation slowed down definitely, but not thrown out. In the end, the Edinburgh Agreement made a few concessions to Danish public opinion, and the Danes gave in, voting 'yes' by 57–43.

Maastricht was difficult, but not an isolated case. In 2001, the Irish rejected the Nice Treaty by the substantial margin of 54-46, though on a low turnout of 35% (this was the only European country that put the Nice Treaty to a referendum). Again it was told to go away and think about it, and not to come back until there was a 'yes'. The adjustments to the treaty were minimal, and the Irish establishment, far from respecting the declared wishes of the voters, poured more effort into getting the vote right. The Fianna Fail Government of the day, having spent €60,000 in the 2001 referendum, spent €500,000 in 2002. The 'yes' vote duly arrived, 63–37.

Is it possible for a referendum to change anything in this context? Yes it certainly is, as the 2005 votes on the EU constitution proved. A number of countries planned to put the constitution to a referendum; some of those referendums were anticipated to be tricky. Britain's was to be the trickiest of all.

The mutual dislike and distrust between Tony Blair and Jacques Chirac is legendary, and it was typical of Chirac to try to use the constitution debate to discomfit his rival. Consequently, he announced an early referendum — which, like Mitterand in 1992, he didn't have to call — in order to put pressure on Blair, who was intent on delaying any British referendum as long as he could. Chirac called the referendum because he knew he could win it — opinion polls had shown a robust 60–40 'yes' lead for several months.

We know a song about that, don't we?

The French rejected the constitution in May 2005, followed a few days later by the Dutch — the first time that they had ever been consulted about the Union. That rejection in two founder members by big majorities on reasonable turnouts was just about enough to put the constitution on ice. Even so, we should not overestimate the extent to which politicians will welcome direct democracy breaking out. There were several calls in the immediate aftermath of the Dutch and French votes for the issue to be put before the people again (vote until you get it right).

The biscuit was well and truly taken by the Prime Minister of Luxembourg, Jean-Claude Juncker, who happened to be the President of the EU at the time. He announced, in all seriousness, that he did not believe that the French or Dutch voters had rejected the EU constitution! That is the classic reduction of the significance of a referendum to something entirely containable within understandable elite politics. Only a 'yes' vote was possible or legitimate; a 'no' vote — inimical to political common sense! — had to be rationalised away as an expression of something else. He went on to hold the Luxembourg referendum on the constitution a few weeks later (which he won — and presumably interpreted as acceptance of the constitution).

Chapter Ten

The Aftermath II

Referendums and the Constitution

Did the Floodgates Open?

The national referendum of 1975 changed the constitution. But was the effect lasting? Well, the answer to that is a firm 'yes and no'. The device of a referendum gave politicians another string to their bows. On the other hand, not many have actually been called. And until the modernising Government of Tony Blair, with its strong focus on legitimacy, creating coalitions, carrying the people with it, opinion polls, focus groups etc, they were used very sparingly indeed.

In fact, they fall into two groups, which we might discuss separately: those to do with alterations to the geography of the British constitution (i.e. who governs whom where), and with Europe. The former group of referendums tends to have been implemented, though not necessarily with happy results, and not nationwide. The latter group take place in imagination only.

Devolving Power (or Not)

The Wilson Government had found the referendum a useful device for holding together a fragile coalition in 1975; it had also wounded the troublesome Tony Benn. But by-elections took their toll of Labour's tiny majority. Appropriately, it was Roy Jenkins who turned majority into minority. By 1977, the new Prime Minister was Jim Callaghan, and his majority had fallen to 1; he had shored up his position by forming an unpopular arrangement with new Liberal leader David Steel (the Lib-Lab Pact). Home Secretary Jenkins took the post of President of the European Commission, which meant quitting the Commons. Jenkins' majority of 12,000 in his Stechford constituency was turned over by the Tories with a 17% swing.

Callaghan found himself running a hugely unpopular minority Government, with Mrs Thatcher constantly on the prowl in the background. Minority parties, holding the balance of power, were in a strong position. Callaghan seized on the referendum device once more to square the circle. The Scottish and Welsh nationalists were campaigning hard for devolution; they were not totally out of sympathy with the Government, but they demanded a *quid pro quo* for their support. On the other hand, Labour had fought hard against devolution in both Scotland and Wales for many years; reversing that stance was hard.

Could the referendum, as a device for allowing one to say different, incompatible things to different people, come to the rescue? Anthony King had advocated exactly this in his 1977 book on the EEC referendum: "The referendum had worked; it had gone smoothly. The genie had been let out of the bottle, and nothing very terrible had happened … The obvious immediate candidate for a further referendum … was the political future of Scotland and Wales."

No-one seriously thought that the Labour Party would split over devolution as it had threatened to over Europe. The more difficult problem for Callaghan was getting legislation through the house. Promising referendums in Scotland and Wales on devolution would keep the nationalists onside, at least in the short term. A yes vote in those referendums would help spike the guns of the anti-devolution Labour MPs; a no vote would weaken the nationalists. And as a final pleasing thought, Callaghan knew his Government was so weak that it couldn't last long enough to put the devolution legislation onto the statute book. If he was turfed out of office, the new Thatcher Government might be in the position of having a sufficient majority to enact devolution legislation, a pair of positive referendum results, but no inclination to break Westminster's hold over the politics of the United Kingdom. The result would be frustration with the Tory government in Scotland and Wales, which would translate into more votes for Labour.

But King was wholly wrong in his analysis. Although it would not show for a while yet, the genie had caused havoc. The 1975 referendum had gone exactly according to plan and had not saved the Labour Party from splits and internecine warfare. The 1979 referendums didn't even go according to plan. In Wales, the no vote was overwhelming, 80–20 on a 59% turnout. But in Scotland there was horrible trouble.

Callaghan's cunning plan to outflank the anti-devolution forces was, of course, obvious to all at the time. And they outflanked him instead. Dissident Labour MPs sided with the opposition to force through what became known as the Cunningham amendment which stated that, in order for a pro-devolution vote to be counted legitimate, not only would there have to be a majority of the votes cast for devolution, but they would also have to constitute 40% of the eligible electorate. The post-referendum debate would have been tricky anyway, as the yes majority was small, 52–48, but the Cunningham amendment caused it to fail, as only 32.9% of the electorate had voted 'yes'. The amendment also caused a great deal of confusion about interpreting the results, as it wasn't clear whether someone's abstention was due to apathy or opposition to devolution (not voting in effect counted as a vote against devolution). The no camp even argued that though they had lost the popular vote, it was close enough to imply that had the Cunningham amendment not been in place more opponents of devolution would have felt obliged to vote 'no', which would have overthrown the 'yes' majority. Clear as mud.

The SNP felt, not unreasonably, betrayed by the system; there had been a referendum on their pet policy, which they had won, but a traitor (George Cunningham was a Scottish MP for a London constituency) had stabbed them in the back with his sneaky Sassenach rules. The politics of victimhood took over, and the nationalists ceased to co-operate with the government. Thatcher took her chance and called a vote of confidence, which she won by one vote. The devolution referendums took place on March 1st, to preserve the Labour government for as long as possible. By May 3rd Mrs Thatcher was Prime Minister. The referendum curse had struck again.

The Tories, who had benefited so much from Labour's use of referendums, were not so stupid to try them, even had Thatcher felt the need to consult anyone other than herself. But Tony Blair quite liked them. Devolution, a rather tiresome policy that Blair had inherited from John Smith, eventually arrived via a referendum. The Scots voted unambiguously for an assembly, 74–26 (64–36 wanting it to have tax-raising powers). The Welsh, on the other hand, produced perhaps the most ambiguous result ever in the history of referendums. On a turnout of 50.1%, they voted yes by 50.3% to 49.7%. In other words, only half the Welsh could be bothered to vote, and of those, only half were in favour of devolution. The Welsh assembly meets with that endorsement ringing in its ears. Londoners were also given the opportunity to vote for a mayor by referendum, which they did by 72–28 on a small turnout, but Labour didn't profit.

More mayoral referendums have been held in various cities; these have been patchily successful (12 yes votes out of 32 held). A man who dressed, professionally, as a monkey became the mayor of Hartlepool, while a man called Robocop has managed to raise Middlesbrough's profile. Most recently John Prescott's pet idea of regional assemblies in England was trounced in the North East, by 78–22, which killed off the policy without Blair having to apply the fatal blow himself.

Promises, Promises ...

Referendums tend to be used in two ways. First, they allow you to avoid a strong identification with your own policies, which means you can say different things to different interested parties. And second, they allow you to buy the support of people whose policies you abhor. If you intend to hold a referendum, then these benefits come with political risk. You have to come off the fence at some point. And, more obviously, you might lose. The referendum is a much more effective device if you have no intention whatsoever of holding one, or if you can put off holding one until the problem has gone away.

Labour's 1997 manifesto began by fretting about cynicism and distrust of politics. There were few grosser breaches of faith than Major's misrepresentations of his policies in his 1992 manifesto, it thundered. It then went on proudly to boast of Labour's commitment 'to a referendum on the voting system in the House of Commons'; this voting system, to remind you, being the one which requires the Tories to have a lead of 11.5% in order to win a majority of one seat. A proportional alternative was to be proposed and voted on. The proposal was duly made, by a commission headed by Jenkins the mould-breaker himself. We still wait for the commitment to be fulfilled, although it would be cynical and distrustful to suggest that, now Labour benefits so handsomely from the system, it never will be. But hope of a referendum kept Paddy Ashdown's Liberal Democrats to heel for a while.

Referendums are wonderful ways of getting you off the hook, and putting your opponents on it. No important referendum took place in Britain during the period of John Major's premiership (1990–97). But you could write a history of that unhappy time in terms of referendums promised. There were many calls for referendums on the

Maastricht Treaty even while it was being negotiated, in 1991. When it was being debated and ratified in Parliament, no less than Thatcher herself demanded one.

The Tories debated the question of whether to have a referendum on the single currency for a long time in the mid-90s, before Major decided to put on record his support for one. The opposition had promised one, from their position of no power whatsoever, purely to put pressure on Major at his weakest point. Political expediency was the only reason given for Major's change of mind; there was not even a pretence of principle about the decision. The Cabinet opponents of a referendum, Kenneth Clarke and Michael Heseltine, rehearsed the well-known arguments against the referendum's anomalous position in a representative democracy. Whether they were also influenced by the thought that they probably couldn't win such a referendum is a different matter. And if Major thought that offering a referendum could neutralise James Goldsmith and his Referendum Party, he had another think coming. Goldsmith trousered the concession and demanded a re-run of 1975.

Blair has been somewhat more adept at managing referendum promises. The 1997 manifesto reiterated Labour's promise of a referendum on the single currency, but cleverly hedged the whole thing so that no-one would believe that such a thing might happen. The Cabinet had to agree first, and then Parliament, and only then would the people be consulted. Gordon Brown then came up with five tests of whether Britain's economy was sufficiently in step with Europe's to justify joining; since none of the tests was terribly precise, that meant that the decision as to whether the criteria had been met were Brown's alone, which in effect gave him something not far off a veto.

The next big proposal for change was Giscard d'Estaing's EU constitution. Blair spent an awful lot of time arguing that the constitution merely wound up a few loose threads, and that it was of much less moment than Thatcher's Single European Act or Major's Maastricht Treaty, each of which had been ratified without a referendum. In April 2004, he changed his mind about the referendum, while explaining in great detail that he hadn't changed his mind about all the reasons previously given *not* to have a referendum. The real reason, one suspects, is that until April 2004, it looked as if neither Spain nor Poland would give way on the issue of voting rights, and that the constitution would not be agreed. But when a compromise was worked out, the constitution was suddenly a serious runner again. And Blair proved as unable to resist the pressure from the Eurosceptic press as Major.

His bacon was saved by the blundering Chirac, who accidentally gave the French people the early opportunity to discard Giscard, which they did. But the referendum calls, as before, were *Realpolitik*, no more, no less.

Dead Horses

I am reminded of an old story. An elderly stablehand is told by the King to teach his favourite horse to talk within a year; if not, he would be executed. The stablehand smiles, and promises enthusiastically that the horse would be conversing on that day's anniversary. When his friend asks how he could so cheerfully have made his impossible promise, the stablehand says: "Plenty can happen in a year. The horse may die. The king may die. I may die. Or the horse may talk."

Relevance? One of the heroes of our story, Harold Wilson, famously remarked that a week was a long time in politics. After the passage of enough time, what seemed like a pressing problem is just a piece of quaint history. And the promise of a referendum can buy enough time for problems to pass away, while giving the impression that the government is doing something about them. When Blair announced the referendum on the EU constitution, no-one—least of all Blair—imagined that the Dutch and French voters would get him off the hook, but they did.

And if the problem doesn't vanish, then a referendum can be used to pass the responsibility for making an awkward decision. John Prescott's referendum on the North East Regional Assembly was Blair's concession to Prescott on a policy on which he was neutral or mildly hostile; the referendum had the right result for Blair if not Prescott. Callaghan's devolution referendums enabled him to make the concessions to the nationalists necessary to keep his minority Government going, without reversing Labour's anti-devolution stance. The single currency and the EU constitution both promised to be sticky issues for British Prime Ministers, but the promise of a referendum staved off immediate trouble; time killed off the danger in the longer term.

The only national referendum Britain has ever held was an overwhelming and supposedly decisive victory for the pro-Europeans. It took under six years for the party which implemented it to fall apart over the issue, seventeen years for the party whose achievement it confirmed to do the same, twenty-two years before another party fought a general election with the single policy of rerunning it. If the 1975 referendum didn't prove decisive, how can it be hoped that any controversial issue can be settled by the device?

There are many arguments about direct democracy — pro or anti. The decision to hold a referendum, history shows, is unconnected to these arguments. Referendums are held by desperate people who wish to retain credibility with incompatible groups, and who want to avoid taking decisions. Whether such a get-out should be available in a representative democracy, which if it is about anything is surely about people deliberating carefully and taking informed decisions on our behalf, is another matter.

In the Internet age, consulting large numbers of people instantly and cheaply is increasingly possible. Snapshots of public opinion can be acquired with online voting. Furthermore, as overt trust in politicians and politics (and journalists, for that matter) has declined, and as cynicism is becoming the norm, we are likely to come under more pressure for more 'consultation exercises'.

There is no particular reason to think that 'the people' will make, on the whole, worse decisions than politicians (or better ones, for that matter). But a look back at 1975 shows us that there is no reason either to think that the decisions thus reached will have any greater legitimacy or longevity than those reached in the House of Commons. If a decision taken by referendum goes wrong, then there is no government sponsor to reject, no alternative party to elect, no way of adjusting the quality of government in response to the failure.

And in a representative democracy, it is the representatives that hold all the cards; they frame the debate, theirs are the only opinions that matter (as argued by Robert Worcester), they decide which questions are put to the people, and which reserved for Parliament. This is not in any sense a move towards direct democracy and genuine consultation. It is the decentralisation of blame, and the evasion of responsibility.

Further Reading

I have used a number of sources while writing this essay. Indeed, I claim very little originality here except with respect to the arrangement of the arguments and evidence, and, of course, in the application of those arguments to Britain's constitutional position in 2006. For the fullest, most valuable and best documented account of the 1975 referendum, see:

David Butler & Uwe Kitzinger, *The 1975 Referendum*, 2nd edition, Basingstoke: Macmillan, 1996.

Some of the other more immediately useful sources are as follows. As I mentioned in the text itself, I do not pretend for a second that this is an exhaustive list.

Mark Baimbridge (ed.), *The 1975 Referendum on Europe Vol.1: Reflections of the Participants*, Exeter: Imprint Academic, 2006.
Mark Baimbridge, Darren Darcy & Andrew Mullen, *The 1975 Referendum on Europe Vol.2: Current Analysis and Lessons for the Future*, Exeter: Imprint Academic, 2006.
Arthur Balfour, *January 1910 Election Address*, http://www.conservativemanifesto.com/1910/jan/january-1910-conservative-manifesto.shtml, 1910.
Barbara Beck, 'A special case', *The Economist*, 12th Feb, 2004.
David Beetham, *The Legitimation of Power*, Basingstoke: Palgrave, 1991.
Nora Beloff, *The General Says No*, Harmondsworth: Penguin, 1963.
Tony Benn, *Against the Tide: Diaries 1973-6*, London: Hutchinson, 1989.
David Butler & Austin Ranney (eds.), *Referendums: A Comparative Study of Practice and Theory*, Washington DC: American Enterprise Institute for Public Policy Research, 1978.
John Campbell, *Edward Heath: A Biography*, London: Jonathan Cape, 1993.
Conservative Party, *A Better Tomorrow: The Conservative Manifesto 1970*, http://www.conservativemanifesto.com/1970/1970-conservative-manifesto.shtml, 1970.
John Dunn, *Setting the People Free: The Story of Democracy*, London: Atlantic Books, 2005.
Mark Garnett & Richard Weight, *Modern British History: The Essential A-Z Guide*, London: Jonathan Cape, 2003.

Sarah Hogg & Jonathan Hill, *Too Close to Call: Power and Politics – John Major in No. 10*, London, Little, Brown, 1995.
Roy Jenkins, *A Life at the Centre*, London: Macmillan, 1991.
Anthony King, *Britain Says Yes: The 1975 Referendum on the Common Market*, Washington DC: American Enterprise Institute for Public Policy Research, 1977.
H.D.F. Kitto, *The Greeks*, Harmondsworth: Penguin, 1951.
Labour Party, *The Labour Party Manifesto 1983*, http://www.labour-party.org.uk/manifestos/1983/1983-labour-manifesto.shtml, 1983.
Labour Party, *Britain Will Win With Labour: The 1987 Labour Party Manifesto*, http://www.labour-party.org.uk/manifestos/1987/1987-labour-manifesto.shtml, 1987.
Labour Party, *New Labour Because Britain Deserves Better: Britain Will Be Better With New Labour*, http://www.labour-party.org.uk/manifestos/1997/1997-labour-manifesto.shtml, 1997.
Lawrence LeDuc, *The Politics of Direct Democracy: Referendums in Global Perspective*, Peterborough, Ontario: Broadview Press, 2003.
John Stuart Mill, 'Considerations on representative government' in John Gray (ed.), *On Liberty and Other Essays*, Oxford: Oxford University Press, 1991, pp. 203–467.
Kieron O'Hara, *After Blair: Conservatism Beyond Thatcher*, Cambridge: Icon Books, 2005.
Kieron O'Hara & David Stevens, *inequality.com: Power, Politics and the Digital Divide*, Oxford, Oneworld, 2006.
Onora O'Neill, *A Question of Trust*, Cambridge: Cambridge University Press, 2002.
Peter Paterson, *Tired and Emotional: The Life of Lord George Brown*, London: Chatto & Windus, 1993.
Ben Pimlott, *Harold Wilson*, London: Harpercollins, 1992.
Enoch Powell, *The Common Market: The Case Against*, Kingswood: Elliot Right Way Books, 1971.
Enoch Powell, *A Nation or No Nation? Six Years in British Politics*, Richard Ritchie (ed.), London: Batsford, 1978.
Richard Ritchie (ed.), *Enoch Powell on 1992*, London: Anaya, 1989.
Douglas E. Schoen, *Enoch Powell and the Powellites*, London: Macmillan, 1977.
Anthony Seldon with Lewis Baston, *Major: A Political Life*, London: Weidenfeld & Nicolson, 1997.
Harold Wilson, *The Labour Government 1964–1970: A Personal Record*, London: Weidenfeld & Nicolson and Michael Joseph, 1971.
John Wood (ed.), *Powell and the 1970 Election*, Kingswood: Elliott Right Way Books, 1970.
Robert M. Worcester, *How to Win the Euro Referendum: Lessons From 1975*, London: Foreign Policy Centre, 2000.

Index

Agriculture, 5, 7, 8, 60, 76, 94
  Common Agricultural Policy (CAP), 10, 11, 18, 43, 48, 79, 94
  Food prices, 43, 48, 59, 60, 67, 79, 83, 90
Algeria, 7, 30
Anti-Common Market League, 61
Ashdown, Paddy, 105
Athens, 32
Attlee, Clement, 5, 28

Balfour, Arthur J., 28
Bank of England, 75
Barber, Anthony, 21
Beetham, David, 32
Belgium, 5, 13, 30, 79
Benn, Hilary, 64, 69
Benn, Tony (Anthony Wedgwood Benn), 21, 23, 25, 26-7, 55, 56, 59, 60, 61&n, 64-5, 66, 67, 69, 71, 74, 75, 76, 77, 78, 79, 80-1, 81n, 82, 83, 86, 87, 88, 89, 90, 91, 96-8, 102
  Bennites, 65, 96-8
  Family, 64
  Personal attacks on, 74, 75, 76, 77, 78, 81
Bevan, Aneurin, 25, 66
Beyen, Jacques, 5
Blair, Tony, 29n, 31, 37-8, 43, 98, 101, 102, 104-5, 106-7
Bob Jones University, 67
Border Region, 85
Bradley, Tom, 97
Britain in Europe (BIE), 49-51, 53, 55, 56, 61, 63, 73, 74, 75, 77, 78, 79, 80, 82, 90, 96-7
British Business for World Markets, 61&n
British Leyland, 79
Brocklebank-Fowler, Christopher, 97
Brown, George, 9, 13-15, 19, 23, 56, 58, 78, 81

Brown, Gordon, 106
Butler, R.A.B., 9

Callaghan, James, 23, 24, 40, 42, 55, 58, 67, 68, 72, 73, 95, 98, 102-4, 107
Cantley, Mr Justice, 54
'Capitalist club', EEC as, 19-20, 59, 77
Carrington, Lord, 21
Cash, William, 99
Castle, Barbara, 23, 61, 67, 69, 71n, 79, 81, 82, 83, 88, 89
Charlemagne, 4
Chirac, Jacques, 6, 101, 107
Churchill, Sir Winston, 5, 8, 28, 82
Citizens' juries, 34
Clarke, Kenneth, 98, 106
Coalition government, 56, 74, 75, 77-8, 80, 82, 87, 96
Collective responsibility, 42-3, 73-4, 77, 79-80
'Common Market' name, 5, 46
Common Market Safeguards Campaign (CMSC), 61, 62, 68, 69
  Labour Committee for Safeguards on the Common Market, 62
  Labour Euro-Safeguards Campaign, 62
Commonwealth, 6, 10, 13, 43, 48, 73, 74
Communist Party, 62, 63, 73, 75
Communists, *see Communist Party*
Confederation of British Industry (CBI), 50
Conservative Party, 6, 8, 12-13, 17, 19, 20-1, 22-3, 27, 28, 38, 50, 51, 62, 72, 73, 81, 87, 90, 97, 98-9, 106, 107
Conservatives Against the Treaty of Rome (CATOR), 62
Cook, Peter, 31, 54
Couve de Murville, Maurice, 12
Crosland, Anthony, 9, 74
Crossman, Richard, 14

Index

Cunningham, George, 104

Davies, John, 80
Day, Robin, 76, 78
De Gaulle, Charles, 6-7, 12-13, 14-15, 16
Democracy
  Deliberative, 35, 108
  Direct, 30-1, 32, 76, 108
  Representative, 31-2, 33-4, 93, 106, 108
Denmark, 22, 29, 30, 39, 100
Devolution, 102-5, 107
Dicey, A.V., 27
Douglas-Home, Sir Alec, *see Earl of Home*
Du Cann, Edward, 81
Duncan Smith, Iain, 98

Elite domination of politics, 31, 35, 37, 88-9, 93, 99, 108
Emery, Peter, 39
England, 44-5, 63, 84-5
Entry negotiations, British
  1961-3, 10-12
  1967, 14-15
  1970-1, 17-19, 95
  1974-5 (renegotiations), 23-4, 37, 40, 55, 95
European Commission, 10, 18, 74, 76, 78, 79, 80, 82, 89, 102
European Free Trade Area (EFTA), 6, 9, 14
European Movement, 49, 51
European Parliament, 59, 67, 87
European Union Constitution, 1, 13, 106-7
  Dutch and French referendums on (2005), 62, 68, 88, 101, 107

Fareham, 52
Feather, Vic, 55-6, 58, 97
Finland, 30
Food, *see Agriculture*
Foot, Michael, 23, 40, 59, 61, 66, 71, 75, 76, 82, 88, 89, 94, 98, 99
Football, 17, 22
Ford, Gerald, 77
France, 4, 5, 6-7, 11-12, 16, 17-19, 29, 30, 100, 101
Free trade, 5, 6, 60
Frere-Smith, Christopher, 68, 81

Gaitskell, Hugh, 9-10, 13, 25, 53
Gale, George, 59

General elections, 37-8
  1945, 5, 8, 28, 66
  1964, 13
  1970, 17, 24, 53, 65, 78-9, 93
  February 1974, 22-3, 25, 27, 37, 38, 44, 45, 62, 65, 73, 78, 84, 88
  October 1974, 23, 24, 25, 38, 44, 45, 73, 84, 88, 96
  1979, 96, 104
  1983, 96
  1987, 96
  1992, 105
  1997, 99, 105
  2005, 98-9
Germany, 4, 29n, 30, 96
  West Germany, 5, 16, 17
Get Britain Out (GBO), 22, 61, 62, 63, 68, 75, 81
Giscard d'Estaing, Valéry, 13, 23, 76-7, 106-7
Glamorgan, Mid, 85
Glamorgan, West, 85
Goldsmith, Sir James, 99, 106
'Great Powers' theory, 4
Greece, 30
  Ancient Greece, 32
Grimond, Jo, 45, 86
Guggenheim, Charles, 77
Gummer, John Selwyn, 51
Gundelach, Finn, 79
Gwent, 85
Gwynedd, 84

Hague, William, 52, 98
Hailsham, Viscount, 29, 64
Hain, Peter, 78
Hart, Judith, 80
Hattersley, Roy, 80
Hayward, Ron, 73
Healey, Denis, 78
Heath, Edward, 7-9, 10, 12, 13, 16, 17, 18-19, 20, 21-3, 25, 26-7, 37, 52, 54, 55, 58, 65, 68, 73, 74-5, 78-9, 80, 81, 82, 84, 86, 87, 97
Heffer, Eric, 74, 97
Henderson, Douglas, 80
Heseltine, Michael, 98, 106
Hitler, Adolf, 29
Hogg, Quintin, *see Viscount Hailsham*
Home, Earl of, 8, 64, 68
Howe, Sir Geoffrey, 98
Hurd, Douglas, 97

Iceland, 30
Indian Workers Association, 78

Inflation, 38, 43-4, 75, 76
Intervention Board, 76
Ireland, 22, 27, 29, 30, 60, 100
Isle of Wight, 45, 86
Italy, 5, 29n, 30, 77

Jackson, Tom, 56, 58
Jay, Douglas, 59, 62, 68, 80
Jenkins, Clive, 56, 69, 71, 81, 86
Jenkins, Roy, 9, 19, 23, 25, 26-7, 29, 45, 48, 50, 52-3, 55, 56, 57, 58, 61, 77, 78, 80-1, 82, 95, 96-8, 102, 105
Jones, Jack, 69, 71, 97
Juncker, Jean-Claude, 101

Kennedy, John F., 12
Kerr, Anne, 62
King, Anthony, 59, 95, 103
Kinnock, Neil, 98

Labour Party, 6, 9, 12-15, 16, 17, 18, 19, 20, 21, 22-3, 24-5, 26, 28, 38, 39, 44-5, 49, 50, 53, 55, 59, 61, 62, 63, 66, 72-3, 80, 87, 90, 95, 96, 97-8, 99, 103, 104, 107
Lawson, Nigel, 98
Legitimacy, 2, 28, 31-2, 34, 39, 49, 100-1, 102, 104
Leighton, Ron, 62
Lever, Harold, 23, 77
Lib-Lab Pact, 102
Liberal Democrats, 97, 105
Liberal "No" to the Common Market Campaign, 62
Liberal Party, 17, 27, 28, 38, 50, 51, 62, 72, 73, 90, 97
London, 85, 104-5
Luxembourg, 5, 17, 30, 101

Maastricht, Treaty of, 1, 98-100, 106
Mabon, Dickson, 50, 97
Macmillan, Harold, 6, 7, 8, 12, 64, 65, 68, 80, 82
Major, John, 98, 99, 100, 105, 106
Marquand, David, 97
Marten, Neil, 59, 68, 73, 80, 81, 86, 90
Maudling, Reginald, 9, 58, 78, 80, 97
McGovern, George, 77
McNally, Tom, 97
Meacher, Michael, 78
Media
  Press, 22, 50-1, 54, 72, 73, 74, 75, 76, 80, 81, 86, 88, 106
  Television, 41, 76, 77, 80-1, 89-90
Mellish, Bob, 77

Mellor, David, 99
Mill, John Stuart, 31
Mitchell, Austin, 62
Mitterand, François, 100, 101
Monnet, Jean, 4, 10
Mussolini, Benito, 29

Napoleon, 4
National Council of Anti-Common Market Associations, 61-2, 61n
National Economic Development Board, 74
National Front, 62, 75, 78
National Referendum Campaign (NRC), 61-4, 68, 73, 74, 75, 77, 79, 80, 81, 88, 90
National Union of Students, *see* Students
National veto, 5, 12-13, 17, 18
NATO, 59
Netherlands, The, 5, 101
Nice, Treaty of, 100
Northern Ireland, 22, 27-8, 44-5, 51, 60, 63, 67, 85, 88, 90
Northern Ireland in Europe, 51
Norway, 29, 30, 60, 79

O'Neill, Onora, 89
Opinion polls, 18, 19, 25, 26, 40, 44, 46-7, 49, 57-8, 61, 69-71, 76, 78, 83, 84, 89, 91, 93, 102, 108
Orkney & Shetland, 45, 86
Orkneys, 86
Owen, David, 97

Paisley, Ian, 67, 70-1, 89
Paisley Jr., Ian, 67
Pardoe, John, 82
Parliament
  Debates and votes, 18, 19, 20-1, 22, 24-5, 26, 28, 38-9, 42, 43-4, 72, 73, 75, 76, 77, 87, 91, 93, 95, 99, 100, 102-4, 105-6, 108
  Parliamentary sovereignty, 43-4, 48-9, 59-60, 75, 76, 78-9, 81, 90
Participation, 31-2
Patriotism, 50, 51-2, 74-5, 78, 82
Plaid Cymru, 44, 51, 62-3, 90, 103
Poland, 106
Pompidou, Georges, 16, 17, 18-19, 23
Portugal, 5
Powell, Enoch, 22-3, 24-5, 26-7, 40, 59, 60, 62, 65-6, 69, 70-1, 74, 75, 80, 81, 82, 84, 86, 87-8, 89, 93-5, 96
Powellites, 65, 75, 78, 96

Powys, 85
Prentice, Reg, 56, 58, 62, 75, 80, 87
Prescott, John, 105, 107
Pym, Francis, 20, 21, 97

Redwood, John, 70
Referendum (1975), 1-2
　Campaign, 72-83
　Decision to hold, 38
　Expenditure, 41, 49-50, 63, 77, 90
　Government-financed pamphlets, 41-2, 43, 48-9, 59-61, 73, 77, 88
　Labour policy on, 24-7, 36, 37-8
　Legitimacy and turnout, 39, 41, 49, 82, 84-6, 96, 99
　No camp, 40-1, 48-9, 59-71, 72, 77, 89, 90, 96
　Result, 84-6
　Result binding on parliament, Question of whether, 39, 73, 75, 78, 82
　Rules, 38-9, 41, 44-7
　Unsatisfactoriness of, 88-91, 93-5
　Yes camp, 40-1, 48-58, 72, 76, 77, 89, 90
Referendum Party, 99, 106, 107
Referendums in the United Kingdom, 28
　Devolution, Scotland (1979), 103-4
　Devolution, Scotland (1997), 104
　Devolution, Wales (1979), 103
　Devolution, Wales (1997), 104
　Mayoral, Hartlepool (2001), 105
　Mayoral, London (1998), 104-5
　Mayoral, Middlesbrough (2001), 105
　North East Regional Assembly (2004), 105, 107
　Northern Ireland (1973), 27-8
　Promised/suggested but not held, 1-2, 27, 28, 101, 105-7
Rinka, 54
Rippon, Geoffrey, 17, 18, 21, 58, 95
Rise and Rise of Michael Rimmer, The, 31
Rodgers, William, 21, 50, 97
Rome, Treaty of, 5, 10, 23, 29
Roper, John, 97
Ross, Stephen, 45, 86
Ross, William, 80

Sandys, Duncan, 8
Scanlon, Hugh, 69, 71, 97
Scilly Isles, 84
Scotland, 44-5, 51, 60, 63, 85, 103-4
Scotland in Europe, 51

Scott, Norman, 54
Scottish National Party (SNP), 44, 62-3, 80, 90, 103, 104
Sharp, Clifford D., 28-9
Shetlands, 85, 86
Shore, Peter, 60, 67-8, 69-71, 74, 78, 80, 81, 82
Short, Ted, 27
Single currency, 1, 18, 43, 76-7, 93-4, 98, 106, 107
Single European Act (1986), 99, 106
Sinn Fein, 51, 62
Smith, John, 98, 104
Soames, Sir Christopher, 8, 18, 19, 50, 56, 58
Social Democratic and Labour Party (SDLP), 51
Social Democratic Party (SDP), 97
Sovereignty, *see* Parliament
Spain, 5, 106
Steel, David, 56, 75, 80, 85, 102
Sterling, 13, 14, 18, 45, 75
Stevas, Norman St. John, 97
Stewart, Donald, 45, 86
Straw, Jack, 67, 69
Students, 69, 74, 75, 78
Suez crisis, 6, 7, 8
Surrey, 85
Sussex, East, 85
Sussex, West, 85
Sweden, 30, 35-6, 60
Switzerland, 29, 30-1, 32, 36, 39

Thatcher, Margaret, 23, 43, 50, 54, 56, 57, 75, 81, 87, 95, 97, 98, 99, 103, 104, 106
Thomson, George, 17, 50
Thorpe, Jeremy, 54, 58, 81
Trade unions, 21-2, 38, 41, 55-6, 59, 60, 63, 73, 77, 79, 87, 89
　ASTMS, 69
　AUEW, 69
　NUR, 50
　TGWU, 69
　Trade Union Alliance for Europe (TUAE), 50, 55
　Union of Post Office Workers, 56
　USDAW, 50
Turkey, 29, 30
Tyne & Wear, 85

Unemployment, 38, 43-4, 48, 59, 60, 76, 77, 78, 80, 83
United States of America, 7, 12, 30-1, 32, 41, 77

United Ulster Unionist Party, 51, 62, 88

Wales, 44-5, 51, 60, 63, 85, 103-4
Wales in Europe, 51
Western Isles, 45, 85, 86
Westland Affair, 98
Whitehorn, John, 97
Whitelaw, William, 21, 57, 58n, 73, 75, 97
Women Against the Common Market, 62
Williams, Shirley, 23, 50, 54-5, 57-8, 61, 74, 95, 96-7
Wilson, Harold, 10, 13-14, 16-17, 18, 19, 21, 22, 23, 24, 25, 26, 28, 29, 37, 39, 40, 42-3, 45, 50, 53, 54, 55, 58, 61, 66, 67, 69, 72, 73, 74, 75, 76, 77, 78, 79-80, 84, 86, 87, 89, 90, 93, 94, 96, 98, 102, 107
Worcester, Robert, 89, 108
World War I, 4
World War II, 4, 6-7

Yorkshire, North, 85

SOCIETAS: essays in political and cultural criticism

Vol.1 Gordon Graham, *Universities: The Recovery of an Idea*
Vol.2 Anthony Freeman, *God in Us: A Case for Christian Humanism*
Vol.3 Gordon Graham, *The Case Against the Democratic State*
Vol.4 Graham Allen MP, *The Last Prime Minister*
Vol.5 Tibor R. Machan, *The Liberty Option*
Vol.6 Ivo Mosley, *Democracy, Fascism and the New World Order*
Vol.7 Charles Banner/Alexander Deane, *Off with their Wigs!*
Vol.8 Bruce Charlton/Peter Andras, *The Modernization Imperative*
Vol.9 William Irwin Thompson, *Self and Society* (March 2004)
Vol.10 Keith Sutherland, *The Party's Over* (May 2004)
Vol.11 Rob Weatherill, *Our Last Great Illusion* (July 2004)
Vol.12 Mark Garnett, *The Snake that Swallowed its Tail* (Sept. 2004)
Vol.13 Raymond Tallis, *Why the Mind is Not a Computer* (Nov. 2004)
Vol.14 Colin Talbot, *The Paradoxical Primate* (Jan. 2005)
Vol.15 J.H. Grainger, *Tony Blair and the Ideal Type* (March 2005)
Vol.16 Alexander Deane, *The Great Abdication* (May 2005)
Vol.17 Neil MacCormick, *Who's Afraid of a European Constitution* (July)
Vol.18 Larry Arnhart, *Darwinian Conservatism* (September 2005)
Vol.19 Paul Robinson, *Doing Less With Less: Britain more secure* (Nov. 2005)
Vol.20 Alan and Marten Shipman, *Knowledge Monopolies* (January 2006)
Vol.21 Kieron O'Hara, *The Referendum Roundabout* (March 2006)
Vol.22 Henry Haslam, *The Moral Mind* (May 2006)
Vol.23 Richard Ryder, *Putting Morality Back Into Politics* (July 2006)
Vol.24 Alice Andrews, *An Evolutionary Mind* (September 2006)
Vol.25 John Papworth, *Village Democracy* (November 2006)

Public debate has been impoverished by two competing trends. On the one hand the trivialization of the media means that in-depth commentary has given way to the ten second soundbite. On the other hand the explosion of knowledge has increased specialization, and academic discourse is no longer comprehensible. As a result writing on politics and culture is either superficial or baffling.

This was not always so — especially for political debate. The high point of the English political pamphlet was the seventeenth century, when a number of small printer-publishers responded to the political ferment of the age with an outpouring of widely-accessible pamphlets and tracts. But in recent years the tradition of the political pamphlet has declined—with most publishers rejecting anything under 100,000 words. The result is that many a good idea ends up drowning in a sea of verbosity. However the introduction of the digital press makes it possible to re-create a more exciting age of publishing. *Societas* authors are all experts in their own field, but the essays are for a general audience. Each book can be read in an evening. The books are available retail at the price of £8.95/$17.90 each, or on bi-monthly subscription for only £5/$10. Details/updated schedule at **imprint-academic.com/societas**

EDITORIAL ADVISORY BOARD

Prof. Jeremy Black (Exeter); Prof. Robert Grant (Glasgow); Prof. John Gray (LSE); Prof. Robert Hazell (UCL); Prof. Anthony O'Hear (Bradford); Prof. Nicholas Humphrey (LSE); Dr. Efraim Podoksik (Hebrew Univ., Jerusalem)

IMPRINT ACADEMIC, PO Box 200, Exeter, EX5 5YX, UK
Tel: (0)1392 841600   Fax: (0)1392 841478   sandra@imprint.co.uk